BUCCANEER

THE PROVOCATIVE ODYSSEY OF JACK REED
ADVENTURER, DRUG SMUGGLER,
AND PILOT EXTRAORDINAIRE

**JACK CARLTON REED
& MAYCAY BEELER**

BUCCANNER-THE PROVOCATIVE ODYSSEY OF JACK
REED, ADVENTURER, DRUG SMUGGLER, AND PILOT EX-
TRAORDINAIRE.

Library of Congress Cataloging-in-Publication Data
Reed, Jack Carlton
Beeler, MayCay

Buccaneer: The Provocative Odyssey of Jack Reed—Adventurer, Drug
Smuggler, and Pilot Extraordinaire

ISBN 978-1939-5210-8-8

Cocaine Industry—United States. 2. Organized Crime-United States. 3. Medellin Cartel. 4. Cocaine Industry-Colombia. 5. Organized Crime-Colombia.
6. Lehder Rivas, Carlos Enrique. 7. Reed, Jack Carlton, 1930-2009. I.Title

To Phyrne, Jack's sister and oldest friend, who never questioned Jack's lifestyle, and who had always been ready to offer her love and assistance in his times of need.

To Carlos, whom Jack describes as, *"My greatly admired adventure amigo—who tended me like a philosopher father—has my undying respect and gratitude".*

To Sheldon, Jack's *"very exceptional friend"*, who shared eleven years of an amazing adventure that is truly the stuff movies are made of. Jack notes, *"I have not got the words to describe the special love and admiration that I have for her".*

And finally, to Jack, my "Memphis Magic Man"—who bore the unbearable; opened me; taught me the magic of miracles and unfathomable love. Your wisdom regarding taking responsibility for creating your own reality, and philosophy about pampering your senses to obtain the highest quality of life, will sustain me until we meet again. May the endearing magical energy you bestowed upon us for happiness and well-being bless you for eternity. Thank you for the joy of our collaborative efforts in writing this book. And thank you for the privilege of joining you on your extraordinary life path, even if it was at the very end.

-MCB

CONTENTS

Jack Carlton Reed (aka Buccaneer)

Maverick entrepreneur. All-American Southern California boy who grew up to be a professional drug-runner pilot and convicted international cocaine smuggler for the Medellin Cartel. This non-conformist was allergic to the drudgery of the establishment. This prompted him to soar into a controversial career and retire as an expat in a Spartan Robinson Crusoe type lifestyle. His role in the cartel and close friendship with drug baron Carlos Lehder, partner to kingpin Pablo Escobar, would land him behind bars in the longest running drug trial in U.S. history. Carlos went by the nickname, Morgan, and Jack, by the nickname Buccaneer. This is Jack's story.

Carlos Enrique Lehder Rivas (aka Morgan)

German-Colombian drug lord. Associate of Pablo Escobar and notorious Colombian drug czar. Former cell mate and business partner of famed smuggler George Jung, who was portrayed in the blockbuster movie *BLOW* by actor Johnny Depp. Morgan ran a drug smuggling business operation out of the Bahamian out island Norman's Cay. It served as a waypoint and trans-shipment center for cocaine transported by small private aircraft from Colombia to the United States. When Morgan asked Jack to work as his personal pilot, he and Jack became fast friends. An enduring friendship ensued. They ended up as co-defendants in one of the highest profile drug trials of all time. Morgan was the first Colombian drug lord to be extradited to the United States.

Sheldon

Jack's love interest. Young teenage girl who would run off with Jack to join him on the adventure of a lifetime. Their provocative fiery love affair kept them constant companions for eleven years.

Mom

Jack's archenemy. Sheldon's eight times divorced mother who hung out with drug dealers and smugglers that supported her social drug habit. Fed up with her mother's incessant party girl behavior, Sheldon sought out a new life by absconding with Jack.

Stringbean

Pilot/Drug Smuggler. Long-time acquaintance of Jack's. Jack had been instrumental in his learning to fly. Stringbean would introduce Jack to Colombian drug lord, Morgan, aka Carlos Lehder.

Poppa Charley

Drug dealer. Stringbean worked under him, flying contraband as a pilot/smuggler. Poppa Charley was Mom's boyfriend. Delving deep into the Southern California drug culture as a pilot smuggler, Jack met Mom through Papa Charley and Stringbean, and was subsequently introduced to her young teen daughter, Sheldon.

Steve

Jack's friend and fellow drug smuggler

Rob

Jack's friend and dope dealer

Dyan

One-time girlfriend of Rob's, who would become a close friend of Jack's. Dyan would visit Jack and Sheldon on nearly every leg of their adventurous lives.

Russ

Smuggler/pilot who would ride along with Jack to Norman's Cay when Jack delivered a new smuggling plane to Morgan.

Jaime

Close Colombian friend of Morgan and Jack.

Skipper

The Captain who would unsuccessfully attempt to sail Jack and Sheldon from Cartagena, Colombia to the South Pacific—by way of the Panama Canal—in the sailing vessel Serena.

Bill

A newfound friend of Jack's. A "Zonie"—a person who works in the Panama Canal zone. Bill was instrumental in introducing Jack to the splendor of the Caribbean side of Panama, where Jack and Sheldon would eventually settle down.

Ed Ward

The head of a Florida drug smuggling group that ran a pot smuggling operation out of Norman's Cay well before Morgan showed up. Eventually, Ward decided he and his team could make more money smuggling cocaine than marijuana, and joined forces with the Colombian business operation.

Poppi

An influential outlaw of sorts exiled to a primitive area of Panama. Well-known and well-versed in the local native environment and its people, Poppi advised Jack on the ins and outs of obtaining real estate in the area. Provided shelter and support for Jack and Sheldon while they searched for the perfect blue lagoon to build their Spartan hut on.

Trini

Native friend who worked as a caretaker for Jack on his remote homestead in Panama.

Jim

Mom's boyfriend and personal drug dealer who was also an undercover agent for the government.

Norman

Jack and Sheldon's beloved canine companion. He was considered the third member of their unconventional family. The golden retriever who accompanied them on all of their adventures from Norman's Cay to Canada, Colombia to Panama.

Pablo Escobar

Morgan's partner. A founder of the Medellin Drug Cartel. Notorious cocaine trafficker and Colombian drug czar. One of the richest men in the world, best known as a narcoterrorist. Infamous for bloodshed, corruption and intimidation. Seen as an enemy to the U.S. and Colombian governments, Pablo was a hero to the poor in Medellin, distributing money to the down-trodden through various goodwill projects.

Robert W. Merkle, Jr.

U.S. Attorney for the Middle District of Florida. Prosecutor in Jack and Carlos' historic high profile drug trial. This bulldog attorney was well known by the nickname "Mad Dog".

Ernst Mueller

Assistant U.S. Attorney for the Middle District of Florida. Prosecutor who assisted Robert Merkle, then finished Jack and Carlos' infamous trial after Merkle stepped down. Moved up into Merkle's position, and was the head prosecutor in Jack's second trial.

MayCay Beeler

Professional Pilot/Broadcast Journalist. Contacted Jack in prison for research on a TV documentary she was producing about Norman's Cay, the Bahamian staging ground for the Medellin Cartel's cocaine smuggling operation. MayCay would eventually become Jack's biographer, co-author, and last confidante.

TIMELINE

September 30, 1930 — Jack Carlton Reed born San Pedro, California

1950 — Starts a family. One of many marriages and relationships to fail.

1965 — Convicted for counterfeiting foreign obligations (pesos). Jailed at Terminal Island for 90 days.

Aug. 7, 1971 — Sets world land speed records for electric powered cars in the Silver Eagle dragster at Bonneville Salt Flats.

1976 — Meets Sheldon, the young teen daughter of a drug dealer's girlfriend.

1976 — Temporarily moves from Southern California to Park City, Utah

1977   Funds running low. Jack moves back to his home base of Southern California to return to his source of income—smuggling pot out of Mexico as a renegade pilot. Sheldon runs off with Jack against her mother's wishes.

1977   Jack jailed in Utah initially on charges of alleged aggravated kidnapping, which eventually were reduced to custodial interference involving Sheldon. Released after serving time for the misdemeanor.

1978   Delivers a special smuggling plane from Southern California to Norman's Cay in the Bahamas. Recruited as a cocaine smuggling pilot. Works as Morgan's (aka Carlos Lehder's) personal pilot for the Medellin Cartel.

1981-82   Leaves Norman's Cay for good with Morgan for Colombia

1982   Jack settles down/living primitively/ homesteading in a remote part of Panama

Feb. 4, 1987   Jack and Sheldon abducted by the DEA in Panama

Feb.5 —Oct 21, 1987	Jacksonville, Florida—Jack jailed and tried with co-defendant Carlos Lehder on smuggling and conspiracy charges related to the Medellin Cartel while undergoing the longest running drug trial in US history.
Oct. 21, 1987	Officially named a federal inmate in Medium Security Prisons—Atlanta, then the Memphis Federal Correctional Institution.
September 1, 2009	Transferred from Memphis FCI to Butner Federal Medical Center
October 9, 2009	Justice at last

"I like to dream, yes, yes
Right between the sound machine
On a cloud of sound I drift in the night
Any place it goes is right
Goes far, flies near
To the stars away from here

"Well, you don't know what
We can find
Why don't you come with me little girl
On a magic carpet ride

"Well, you don't know what
We can see
Why don't you tell your dreams to me
Fantasy will set you free."

Steppenwolf

A NOTE FROM JACK REED

I'm no God damn rat! I'm a player. I'm a pirate. I'm a hedonist; and one hell of good smuggler, but I'm no rat!

This is the true story of the events of my life. It involves arriving at the infamous Norman's Cay in the Bahamas*, participating in the island drug smuggling business, and the subsequent consequences that include stunning punishment for refusing to rat on my comrade in the courtroom.

*Norman's Cay is an out island 210 miles off the Florida coast in the Bahamas Exuma chain. Having gained notoriety in the late 70's as a staging point for drug smuggling, Norman's Cay was immortalized in "Blow", a 2001 motion picture starting Johnny Depp. From 1978 through 1982, Norman's Cay was the epicenter of the world's largest drug smuggling operation. It was the tropical playground of drug czar Carlos Lehder, partner to Pablo Escobar, founder of the Medellin Cartel. Cocaine was flown in from Colombia by private aircraft, then reloaded into other aircraft, and flown to locations in Georgia, Florida, and the Carolinas. Authorities allege the island operation was responsible for 80% of the cocaine that entered the United States at that time.

"Come on baby, light my fire." –The Doors

JACK REED'S INTRODUCTION

Lust was my nemesis. For as long as I can remember, it lured me. Aroused me. Seduced me. And because it felt so good, I couldn't resist. In all my relationships with the ladies, I strived to not only cultivate, but sustain the titillation. To find a way to make the erotica last indefinitely. To stave off the inevitable—the demise of lust that always occurred after the familiarity of my lover led to boredom—thus, extinguishing the initial flush of carnal desire. After much trial and tribulation, I discovered the secret to making lust last, but lost my freedom along the way. Since I am a convicted drug smuggler, you likely assume contraband was the sole culprit that led to my arrest; however, in looking back, lust was a player. Lust was the leading lady that contributed to my undoing.

This story was written in 2005.* I was born in Southern California in 1930. I might be considered an adventurer by some; by others perhaps—a damn fool. Many of my acquaintances in my present life, upon hearing some of my tales, have suggested that I put pencil to paper and share some of my exploits with those having an adventuresome nature. I'm not sure that my controversial lifestyle is really that interesting to others; however, the idea caught my fancy when I realized that in writing about my adventures, I would be able to relive them by recalling them to memory. This alone was motivation enough to produce the following story. Because this was written for my personal pleasure, embellishing the facts served no purpose. It's a possibility that some of the events might be slightly out of sequence. All of the characters depicted in my story have been called by their first names or nicknames, except where it made no difference. Parts of my story might be sensitive to some. In the parts involving criminal activities, all of the facts are a matter of public record, except for my personal comments and observations.

MAYCAY'S ADDENDUM

*In 2007, I, a TV producer, want to interview Jack Reed, an incarcerated international cocaine smuggler, about being the personal pilot of a drug cartel linchpin. He refuses. He never has, never will grant interviews, having grown sick of media hounding him for his infamous story.

I respect his privacy, but something tells me I really, really should talk to him. I write him back, admitting I don't know why. Restrained from asking the obvious questions about the drug cartel and his role in it, I fall back on what we have in common: we are both experienced pilots. I ask him about his flying adventures.

He tells me. Does he ever. My. Jaw. Dropped. I ask for more, and more. He lets me read his memoirs. But the more I get to know him, the more questions I have about how he, a mom and apple pie all-American boy, turned into a smuggler. He's had twenty years to meditate behind bars, to look deeply into himself, and he's able to answers those questions, too.

I sense almost immediately that he shouldn't be serving a life sentence at all, let alone having been slapped with two. Something is wrong here. How could it happen? How did it happen?

As Jack relates his account of his arrest and trial (the story has never been given to any other journalist), and I learn of the egregious miscarriage of justice for this non-violent offender, I am angered and sickened. I want to scream at the sheer wrongness of it all. But I'm not a lawyer. What can I do?

So close have Jack and I become, so deeply in tune with one another, Jack tells me that I can be his biographer. Now I have a purpose. I know what I am going to do with the reams and reams of exclusive interview notes I have taken that augment the memoir he wrote. I am going to write his story.

I begin the background research and uncover a piece of data. Domino-like, one thing leads to another and another, and suddenly I'm not just recording Jack's story, I am a character in it. I have to take a stand against powerful government agencies. I think standing up might take more courage that I have, but when

I look inside and see how much my heart has opened through knowing Jack, I know that I can, I *will* find the courage.

Buccaneer: The Provocative Odyssey of Jack Reed—Adventurer, Drug Smuggler, and Pilot Extraordinaire is a compilation of the memoirs Jack wrote in prison, and my personal notes taken from exclusive interviews towards the end of his life. As his biographer, I felt it was my job to ensure Jack's life story had a happy ending. It is my privilege to complete Jack's stimulating saga in this biography, —and to not only write, but participate—in the unpredictable epilogue to this maverick entrepreneur's riveting journey that had always been larger than life.

> *"My family knew me as the all-American Pat Boone type lad, but I was overwhelmed by my desire to shed the stereotyped role and pursue a life of adventure and freedom instead. My adventure with Carlos Lehder was a great learning experience and I wouldn't change one second of it."*
>
> *—JCR*

MAYCAY'S PREFACE

When I first corresponded with Jack in prison, he was 77 years young. I was immediately taken aback by his impossibly courteous and kind disposition, not at all what I would expect from an outlaw who had endured over two decades behind bars. I found Jack to be a distinguished gentleman; a wise and tender soul, gifted untrained artist, philosopher, and dedicated student of metaphysics. He told me he was a pacifist and an "*eccentric old pirate*". I couldn't help but wonder what life circumstances had led this gentle non-conformist from his self-proclaimed "*all-American boy*" roots to the controversial life of an international cocaine smuggler for the Medellin Cartel. Jack's early years bore no semblance to the unconventional career and primitive Robinson Crusoe type lifestyle he would later adopt.

Jack was born into a middle class family in Riverside, California. His mother was a homemaker; his father—the foreman in the press room of the local newspaper. Jack was the only son with two siblings, living a modest life in the days when Riverside was rural and agricultural, —no gangs, no drugs, and little crime.

Jack: "*The great depression was still lingering when we kids were living at home – but we were well taken care of by our loving compassionate parents.*"

Jack enjoyed 5 cent McDonald's hamburgers and 10 cent Saturday matinees featuring King Kong and the Wizard of Oz. His childhood interests included gymnastics and springboard diving. As a young man growing up in the era featured in TV's Happy Days, Jack, like the Fonz, and his "hot rod" buddies, donned Levis and leather jackets, sporting duck tail haircuts with lots of grease.

Jack: "*We didn't go to parties and seldom dated girls, and to this day, I might be considered reclusive.*"

In addition to hanging out at the local drive-in, Cole's Corral, acting aloof and drinking cherry cokes, Jack engaged in his favorite pastime—drag racing his homebuilt hot rods on desolate dirt roads. This would spark the notoriety that would come later in life, when Jack moved into top fuel dragsters and set world land speed records in the electric powered Silver Eagle dragster at the Bonneville Salt Flats in 1971. This achievement immortalized Jack in the Smithsonian Institution.

From the Los Angeles Times, Morning Briefing, Saturday, Aug 7, 1971

Jack Reed, 40, of Huntington Beach set a new world record for electric powered cars Friday, pushing his Silver Eagle to a speed of 146.437 mph at Bonneville Salt Flats. The car is powered by 180 silver-zinc cells, the same type of batteries used to power the Apollo 15 Lunar Rover.

In addition to racing, Jack's passions included scuba diving. He was most at home in or near the ocean. Jack's love for the sea motivated him to build his own Aqua Lung out of war surplus parts, since at that time, SCUBA was not yet available in the U.S., having being introduced by Cousteau in France. This led

Jack to Mel Fischer, who owned the closest dive shop, in search of compressed air to fill his tank. Jack and Mel became fast friends, being only two of a handful in the country interested in SCUBA. As an avid diver, Jack spent thousands of hours skin and scuba diving involving much underwater photography and a movie or two. Jack would later work for U.S. divers—Jacques Cousteau's first dive shop in the U.S., and he, himself, would become a pioneer in the SCUBA industry. Of Jack's establishment jobs, it seems this brought him the most joy.

Jack: *"Making money doing what you enjoy is of course the ultimate achievement in the establishment. That is, if you don't mind settling for a so-so quality of life—in lieu of being an adventurer and world traveler."*

Jack's additional conventional jobs would run the gamut from working as an apprentice pressman for his Dad; to subsequent ordinary jobs in auto parts supply; furniture; as a small dive shop operator; UPS driver; and pilot as a partner in an air charter business (Jack describes his clientele as mostly Vegas gamblers, *"A more reprehensible group would be difficult to find!"*). In addition, Jack was driving top fuel dragsters on weekends in the Southwest, *"Mostly for ego fulfillment than for money,"* he admits. Much of this, including his marriage at that time, came to an abrupt end when Jack was jailed at Terminal Island for counterfeiting Mexican pesos.

After his release, Jack eventually became a partner in a successful corporation leasing automatic car wash equipment. That venture grew to include another corporation—this one involving lobster and shrimp fast food take-out meals, with Jack supplying his own product by owning a fishing fleet. *"I wasn't comfortable in a suit and having a suite of offices,"* so Jack moved to Costa Rica and went lobster fishing, shipping the frozen product back to LAX where his partner would sell it to restaurants. Jack was in charge of production, his associate in charge of finances; but this partner had a shady agenda. He swindled Jack out of all his money and the ownership of two corporations. Jack tells me it was this blow that ended his personal attempts *"to survive by honest (most of the time) and socially acceptable endeavors in the system—and because I really did not consider myself an outlaw, I never suffered any remorse and never will. Other than being a liar and a cheat in most of my relationships,* (referring to five failed marriages Jack owns up to as being totally his fault), *I bear no shame for anything that I've done. My inexcusable behavior with the ladies was to satisfy my lustful desires, and I have since learned how to make a relationship work to everyone's heightened and sustained satisfaction."*

The betrayal of Jack's business partner plays a key role in his life story. Jack explains, *"I was a bit irate, but conceded that it was really a blessing, not having hardly any pleasure being a businessman, and an exciting career as a smuggler waiting in the wings".*

CHAPTER ONE

THE BEGINNING OF THE END: ARMED TO THE TEETH

MY STORY STARTS on the 4th day of February, 1987. From memory, I painted the rustic home depicted in this book. I shared this home with my two most cherished companions and various creatures. Sheldon—my young girlfriend and lover, best friend and confidante—hails originally from Southern California. Norman, our beautiful golden retriever, is a native of Florida. He has shared much of the adventure that I am about to relate. Our creature friends consist of what you might expect to find in a tropical rainforest. We co-exist quite nicely.

Our secluded home is located on the primitive Caribbean coast of Panama. We have lived here approximately six years. It has all of the amenities that you would find in a tropical paradise, including a pristine white sand beach and a blue lagoon fringed with coconut palms the trade winds blew through.

It's mid-morning. What few chores I am responsible for have long been completed. I am lounging in my hammock on the porch, enjoying a cup of robust Panamanian coffee. I am trying to decide whether I want to go snorkeling this morning or wait until later in the day. We have a barrier reef on the outer edge of the crystal clear lagoon that our home has been constructed in; the home sitting on stilts a few feet offshore.

Sheldon is off somewhere—likely working in her garden in a different section of our property. Our homestead comprises about ten hectares, which translates to twenty five acres more or less. It is a peninsula with a three hundred foot high ridge running through it, mostly covered with dense jungle. There is an isthmus on the peninsula with a low spot in the ridge. Little vegetation grows here due to the constant trade winds gusting and carrying salt spray from crashing waves on the seaward side of the peninsula. It was in this area that Sheldon, on her way back to our little home, reported seeing some men at the top of the isthmus. She said it looked as if some of them were armed. I was shocked to hear this—because to see anyone on our property, except our native neighbors, was akin to seeing aliens.

It took me about two minutes to reach the area where I had a clear view of the isthmus. I had to traverse the face of a steep cliff behind our home on a narrow path we had excavated to access our beach and other flat sections of the property. Our garden guest house, water wells and other structures were all located in this area.

Now I was confused,not being able to see a soul, but knowing that Sheldon was not playing some kind of practical joke on me. This is not her nature, and there was no doubt about the serious-ness of her report.

It was the next moment that I heard the sound of an outboard motor coming around the point of the peninsula. Not one—but two native Cayucos appeared. These are long slender boats carved out of large trees. Each boat was carrying about eight people that looked like natives dressed in street clothing.

This further confused me, because even though we have been visited on rare occasion by native friends, there had never been more than four or five show up at one time. As the boats negotiated a tricky channel through the reef surrounding our lagoon, I stood on our beach surveying the situation. By now they were close enough where I could see them clearly. I was unable to recognize anyone that I knew.

CHAPTER TWO

ABDUCTED!

THE NEXT MOMENT I received the surprise of my life. As the boats reached the shore, every person onboard stood up with some type of weapon pointed at me. They were screaming in English and Spanish for me to lie down on the beach. About that time, the men that Sheldon had seen came running down the isthmus, armed to the teeth. Some surrounded me; others went off in different directions.

One, who appeared to be the leader of the raid—and who looked and acted like an American—handcuffed me. He took out a photo, glanced at it and looked at me hard, saying that I was the one they were looking for. He identified himself as a special agent for the Drug Enforcement Administration, and told me that I was under arrest. He informed me that I had been indicted in the United States in 1981 for drug related crimes along with my Colombian friend Carlos Lehder. I was told that he had been captured two days earlier in Colombia. Sheldon and I were to be returned to the states, where I would be prosecuted. I was also informed that they had known where I was living for a year and a half, and they didn't bother with me until they captured Carlos, whom he referred to as the "Kingpin" of the Medellin Drug Cartel.

He left Sheldon and me on the beach in the custody of several Panamanians who turned out to be members of Noriega's National Guard. The DEA agent, now accompanied by another agent who arrived at the scene late as the result of falling off the trail leading to our property, proceeded to our home where they ransacked the place. Most of Noriega's people were combing the property looking for contraband I presume. Except for a small stash of pot for my personal pleasure, there was nothing to be found, much to their disappointment I later discovered. They had been looking for a cache of Colombian cocaine and weapons, assuming that I was operating a waypoint for the trans-shipment of drugs from the Cartel in Colombia—through Panama—and as I later learned, to Nicaragua. After thoroughly searching our property, and finding nothing, they realized we were living a Spartan lifestyle that could be likened to the story of Robinson Crusoe.

The DEA, with a few of Noreiga's henchmen, then decided to check out several sailboats in the bay that adjoined our property called PLAYA BLANCA. This is a beautiful bay, and during the cruising season is occasionally used by cruisers—many from Europe—as an option to staying at the busy marina near the entrance to the Panama Canal on the Caribbean side.

I learned that the agents were confident that they would find contraband aboard these vessels, but were once again disappointed after ransacking every vessel anchored in the bay. Later information divulged that the agents subjected the boat occupants to the usual "no knock" procedures that the U.S. government agents are so unpopular for.

After being disillusioned that they had erred in expecting a major drug bust, the agents loaded Sheldon and me into one of their Cayucos. Alas! It was a tearful time to have to say goodbye to our dear canine friend and adventurer Norman, who was left behind to fend for himself. It was a very sad time indeed!

We were shuttled up the coast to a small native village where the raid had been organized. Upon arriving and being placed in one of their vehicles, I was told that their raid was not a total loss—for they had captured me, and I was destined to be the government's "star witness" against my friend Carlos and the Cartel's operations. They had been informed that Carlos was in custody, and I was privy to this information being a close friend of Carlos'. I was also told that if I had any inhibitions about cooperating with the government, I would be put away for a very long time. On the other hand, if I decided to cooperate, there were ways to reward my assistance.

We were driven across the country to Panama City on the Pacific side, a distance of about fifty miles. There we were turned over to Panamanian authorities, with instructions to hold us in-communicado overnight. Sheldon and I slept on the floor in the office of some government building in a remote part of the city. We were awakened by the day crew showing up for work, given some food, and picked-up by the DEA agents. We were driven through back streets to Howard Air Force Base, a U.S. military installation. The sentry on duty waved our vehicle through. We drove several minutes across the tarmac and pulled up alongside a plane with one of its two engines running. I recognized the plane as a Merlin, a long-range high performance turboprop. It had U.S. civilian registration numbers.

I later learned this was a DEA plane that had been confiscated from drug smugglers. It had been flown down from the states the night before to transport us back. In order to make it look like we weren't being kidnapped, the DEA had two Panamanian police accompany us on the trip back. When we arrived in Jacksonville, Florida, it would appear to those waiting that we had been ousted by the Panamanians and turned over to the U.S. authorities in Florida.

CHAPTER THREE

THE LURE: FORBIDDEN FRUIT, POT AND FAST MONEY

FLASHBACK ELEVEN YEARS—"STRINGBEAN" is a long -time acquaintance I had been associated with many years before the start of this adventure, which commenced sometime in the mid-seventies. Having been affiliated with a small air charter business, I had become a pilot in the early sixties and had been an influence on Stringbean's learning to fly. He used his skills basically to smuggle Mexican pot into Southern California where we both resided. While I initially used my flying skills in honest work; I, too, would become a pot smuggler.

At this particular point in time, Stringbean was flying for a dealer called "Poppa Charley". Stringbean introduced me to Poppa and his girlfriend that I will refer to as "Mom". She and I lived in the same neighborhood of Huntington Beach. Mom was a flamboyant lady who loved to party, do drugs socially, and hang out with drug dealers and smugglers. Long -term relationships were difficult for her to maintain, having been married eight times and giving birth to three children. One of her children was Sheldon.

Mom had an outgoing personality and was for the most part a pleasure to be around. That is, unless you were unfortunate enough to fall out of grace with her for almost any reason; at which time, she would snap, and turn into a vicious junk yard dog. Although I was not attracted to her as a woman sexually, I liked her as a person, and found myself dropping by her home on occasion to smoke a joint and be amused by her outrageous stories.

I became acquainted with her children, Sheldon being the oldest. Sheldon was a cute young teen—petite, with long brown hair and pretty blue eyes. I thought she was charming and looked forward to chatting with her on my visits. It soon became clear that she was very displeased with her mother's lifestyle and choice of friends—myself being the exception. She thought I was a nice old guy who treated her much better than her eight times divorced mother.

When I met Sheldon, the only thing she knew how to do was chew bubble gum and eat sunflower seeds. She was fourteen years old at the time; thirty-two years my junior. Perhaps due to the tawdry environment her mother subjected her to, Sheldon seemed older than her years.

Her home smelled of sweetish weed smoke mixed with the yeasty tang of empty beer bottles. It's an aroma I've come to associate with this caliber of business. Not bad people, just not as cultured as one would like to associate with on a regular basis. In a shadowed living room, one of the only rooms in the house that is blessedly air conditioned, I first noticed Sheldon lounging on the couch. The air was so cool her little breasts pressed hardened nipples against the threadbare T-shirt she had clearly outgrown. If she noticed I was looking at her chest in an inappropriate manner she gave no indication, as she popped her gum while watching me interact with Mom and Poppa Charley. Sheldon would twirl her gum on her finger and engage in frivolous chit chat. The topics she flitted across were lost to the simple naive innocence of her demeanor coupled with her young supple body. It radiated sensuality with a refreshing unconsciousness, filling me with wildly inappropriate thoughts about young Sheldon. She was a blank canvas, completely unaware of everything that was out there to discover with the right partner. I could instill her with a life's worth of knowledge while at the same time enjoying her youthful body as I taught her to explore every aspect of lust and satisfaction imaginable.

At the onset, our budding relationship may have been considered improper or forbidden; but frankly, the age difference between Sheldon and me only created a problem when we occasionally had to deal with the establishment's culturally biased dogma. Friends and acquaintances were on the same frequency as Sheldon and me.

Looking back, Sheldon was never young or beautiful (for long) having grown up quickly by running off with me. Upon my initial introduction to Sheldon, I never could have imagined that within a year, I would begin an expatriate lifestyle and ask her to join me. I told her that to join me on this adventure she had no obligation except be my friend, and anytime that she grew uncomfortable with our relationship, I promised to send her wherever she wanted to go. Thus, our relationship would develop and flourish in an anti-establishment environment where we were to become constant companions for eleven years, and would likely still be except for my existing creation (prison). I give credit to our successful relationship to the anti-establishment lifestyle and the provocative intimacies that we pursued together, creating a bond that was unimaginable in all my establishment relationships.

CHAPTER FOUR

PARK CITY

SOMETIME AFTER MEETING Sheldon, while she was still living at home, I decided I had had my fill of Southern California and needed a change of scenery. It was the beginning of summer, and Stringbean suggested it was the perfect time to take a trip to Park City, Utah, to visit one of his favorite ski resorts. Hardly anyone would be in town this time of year, and a rental would be easy to negotiate for the forthcoming season. A great idea I thought. We packed-up, lock, stock and barrel, and headed north, Stringbean in his Mercedes, and I in my El Camino. Just as he predicted, we found several options available. Stringbean leased a condo for a year, and I leased a small cabin next door called "The Happy Hut".

We spent the summer there, getting acquainted with the few remaining locals. I kept in touch with a few acquaintances in Southern California, Mom being one of them. After learning of our move, she was eager to check out this newfound playground. In doing so, she ended up loving it, making arrangements to rent a place for herself.

There were three new participants I met in Park City that were to become involved in my adventure. Steve was a quiet personable young man who hailed from Colorado. An avid skier, he had moved here to work in a local ski shop to support himself. He occupied a small room behind the shop.

Other participants included Rob and Dyan from Southern California who had moved to Park City to work, ski, and party. They were a handsome young couple that lived together on the outskirts of town in a small old house. Rob was a waiter in a local restaurant and sold a little dope on the side. Dyan hustled drinks in a local pub to supplement their income. Rob was a likeable sort, but never became as good a friend as Dyan, who would often accompany me on the medium ski trails which I finally learned to master. Dyan was an excellent skier and cut a fine figure on the slopes.

I'm not a party person, and spent most of the winter on the slopes practicing, or in my cozy little hut smoking pot and listening to music. Being neighbors, Stringbean and I saw each other regularly, often eating meals together at one of the local eateries. My comfy little Happy Hut had many visitors during my stay at Park City.

When Mom came to stay at the end of the summer, she brought Sheldon with her. It wasn't long before Mom made quite an impression on the locals and dove deep into the drug and party scene. She and Stringbean spent much time together while I showed Sheldon the splendor of the forests and mountains surrounding us. Winter arrived – the beautiful people arrived—and the snow came. The party was on!

Mom would party all night and sleep all day which was her normal routine. Sheldon and I became close friends and discussed future plans. Being fed up with Mom's partying lifestyle,

Sheldon was contemplating moving in with a friend in Southern California.

My lease would be expiring soon. The beautiful people eventually moved to warmer climates, including Stringbean and the rest of my Park City friends. I had no plans. Mom was irritated with me for paying too much attention to Sheldon. She acted jealous. Sheldon made up her mind to leave and strike out on her own. Steve had found a new job in Montana. I contacted him and asked if Sheldon could stay with him until I could personally see to it that she got back to Southern California. Mom had forbid her to associate with me, as I, unfortunately, had made Mom's list of undesirables. I flew from Utah to Montana, met Steve and Sheldon and made arrangements for a flight to Southern California for Sheldon. The plan was to meet her at LAX, after returning to Park City, settling my affairs, and driving back to Los Angeles. Everything went off as planned. The Park City episode of my adventure was over. Or so I thought.

CHAPTER FIVE

WANTED!

BACK IN CALIFORNIA, Sheldon stayed with me while trying to decide if she wanted to move in with a girlfriend. I contacted Rob, who had also returned here, after having split up with Dyan. He informed me that the FBI had been by just the day before looking for me. It seems that after Sheldon left Park City, and I disappeared shortly thereafter, Mom put two and two together and went into a rage. She advised everyone left in town that "she was going to hang my ass"! She went to the local police and swore out a complaint that I had forcefully kidnapped her daughter, and the hunt was on. Suspecting that I had fled the state of Utah, the FBI was called in on the case. Sheldon called a relative who confirmed it was true. They were looking for both of us.

All of my life I have dreamed of living on a beautiful tropical island in the South Pacific. This seemed like an ideal time to check this out. The only place with a name I could remember there was Pago Pago, having seen a movie years before, possibly with Humphrey Bogart. As it turned out, Pago Pago is a small village on the island of Tutuila in American Samoa. I decided to give it a shot. Sheldon wanted to go with me. I booked us a flight on a PAN AM 747 to paradise.

The island was pretty enough, but we discovered the American Samoans were not particularly fond of Americans, only for the welfare checks they received monthly from the U.S. Treasury Department. Ironically enough at the time, we were detained at the airport of entry, suspected of smuggling drugs into their country. We were the only Americans to arrive on this particular flight. Rude treatment and high prices put a damper on any thoughts of staying more than a couple of weeks. We decided to pack up and return to where we had more resources and knew our way around.

Southern California being the likely place where the police were looking for us, we decided to fly to Georgia to visit an old race car driving buddy of mine and take a look at the lay of the land.

This turned-out to be an imposition on him and his family, so we returned, once again, to Southern California. I purchased some cheap transportation, as funds were getting low, and we moved into a cheap sleazy motel in a little country town called Sunnymead. Having run out of money and ideas, I got a job as a fry cook at a local truck stop, using a fictitious name. I had only worked there a short time when the FBI showed up and arrested me. They found Sheldon at the motel and turned her over to her mother and stepfather-whom Mom had reunited with since returning from Park City.

The agents told me the description and photo of a WANTED person were always posted in law enforcements agencies in and around the person's hometown. Fugitives frequently return to familiar territory—family and friends, as it happened in my case. I was recognized by a Highway Patrolman who routinely stopped by for lunch at the café where I worked.

I was kept in the Riverside County Jail until arrangements could be made to extradite me back to Utah where the charges were pending. The FBI, having determined the truth of the matter, dropped their interest in the case; however, I was being detained on a charge of Aggravated Kidnapping—a serious felony. Stringbean came to visit me with news that, according to his attorney, I could be facing thirty years in prison. I soon discovered the common belief that you're innocent until proven guilty should be placed in the category of tales that begin with "once upon a time". The seriousness of my charge, to my dismay, dictated that I be held in maximum security and treated accordingly.

The only two cops in Park City during the off season showed up to transport me back to Utah by car. I knew them both, and they showed some sympathy for my situation by making the trip as pleasant as possible. I was deposited in the Salt Lake County Jail, since there were no facilities in Park City for holding me until trial.

More than six months passed until my day in court arrived. I was transported by the same two cops to a makeshift court where I was appointed an attorney to represent me. He informed me that Sheldon and her parents had come to testify. Sheldon had made it perfectly clear that I had not kidnapped her; that she had run away from her mother whom she considered a bitch. Sheldon had planned to testify in court, under oath, that her mother had lied to the police about the entire incident.

My attorney said the judge was willing to make a deal. The kidnapping charge would be dropped if I would plead guilty to "Custodial Interference". Somewhat disappointed, I told him that I was not guilty of that either. He then informed me that charges of "Statutory Rape" would be brought against me if I didn't accept the deal. Now I was getting irritated, and told him that couldn't be proven either. My attorney agreed that there was that possibility, but arrangements could be made to keep me in jail for at least a year before the matter was resolved. Now that I understood the rules of the game, I politely asked what the penalty was for custodial interference. It was a third class misdemeanor, which carried a ninety day sentence and a $295 fine. I told him we had a deal! I went before the judge, the deal was made, and I was carted away without ever seeing Sheldon.

Coalville is a small ranch town and the county seat for Park City. This is where I would serve my time. The jail here was built in 1904 and is reputed to have been the home of Butch Cassidy during his heyday.

I was the only prisoner, except on weekends, when a drunk or two might be held overnight to sober up. The Sheriff and his deputies owned ranches, and appeared to be more interested in being cowboys than cops. I conducted myself like a gentleman, and they treated me accordingly. Whenever I wished, without supervision, I would help out with yard work at the courthouse. I was taken to the local barbershop, where I was treated like one of the locals. I was even trusted to walk the few blocks back to the jail when I was finished. My treatment was a very pleasant change indeed.

I arranged to have a friend in Park City pay my fine. After about thirty days as the Sheriff's guest, I was told that my being in jail there served no purpose. It was an inconvenience for his deputies to feed and care for me. He said he had called the judge about releasing me, for which I was very happy. The next day, I was delivered to the judge's home, where, as a matter of convenience, he sometimes held court on his back porch. The hearing was casual. He told me if I promised not to return to Park City for one year, he would release me. I promised I would do better than that and stay completely out of Utah! I thanked the judge and the Sheriff for their kind consideration. I was picked-up by friends from Park City and driven to the airport in Salt Lake where they gave me money to catch a flight to Southern California. There, my dear sister, who is my oldest friend, came to my rescue and let me lick my wounds at her home while I got reorganized.

CHAPTER SIX

MOTH TO A FLAME

"Well, you don't know what, we can find, why don't you come with me little girl, on a magic carpet ride. Well, you don't know what, we can see, why don't you tell your dreams to me; fantasy will set you free" —**Steppenwolf**

I **HAD VERY MUCH** enjoyed my relationship with Sheldon. My attraction to her was inescapable. When it came to the ladies, I preferred them young and tender; and if I had a young honey and a bag of weed, I would most certainly indulge. Originally, I must confess, my interest in Sheldon was largely influenced by my lustful attraction to an affectionate young virgin; however, there was something more to Sheldon than the obvious girlish appeal. I cared for her. I was smitten. Like a moth to a flame, I felt compelled to find her, even though I knew there would likely be dues to pay.

I learned that Sheldon and her parents had relocated to Denver. With some apprehension, I called Mom and discovered that her animosity towards me had cooled considerably. She admitted that Sheldon detested her for what she had done to me. Mom suggested that in order to get back in the good graces of her daughter, she would allow Sheldon to see me if I might be interested in moving to Colorado with the hope that seeing each other would reconcile the problem. She even offered to let me stay at their home until I could get enough money to afford my own place. I eagerly agreed, flew to Denver, and was very pleased to see my partner in crime once again. So much so, that the bitterness I had harbored against Mom diminished significantly.

While looking for some type of income, I earned my keep at Mom's place doing odd jobs around the house and yard. I eventually landed a job at an air freight delivery company where I made enough money to buy a worn out Ford station wagon and rent a small apartment. Sheldon and I saw each other whenever possible, but all was not well at Mom's place. Tension mounted between Sheldon and Mom, until Mom told Sheldon to just go ahead and move in with me if she so desired. So she did. This did not sit well with Mom or her husband, although Mom would stop by on occasion to share a joint with me. One day, for no apparent reason, knowing I had some pot in my apartment, Mom called the police and I ended up getting arrested. I was held for a few hours until the secretary where I worked bailed me out. Mom forced Sheldon to return home. Mom's Jekyll and Hyde behavior was getting old. It was a warning of a future fiasco that was gathering speed, rumbling down the tracks towards me like a locomotive. My mind was working overtime, trying to figure out a plan to end this nightmare.

Under constant threats by Mom, Sheldon and I had to sneak around like a couple of thieves in the night to see each other. Our mutual attraction escalated. We both very much wanted to be together, but not under these circumstances. I told Sheldon I had

had enough of Mom's drama. I was going to return to Southern California to reorganize my life. I invited her to join me, but be prepared for some fresh ideas. She enthusiastically agreed, and we planned for our second great escape.

We rented an apartment near LA and I started contacting old business acquaintances from earlier pot smuggling ventures. It was time to make some money and increase my quality of life!

Before meeting Sheldon, I had been a failure with the ladies. I was a liar, a cheat, and a playboy. I tried and tried to live out the customary roles society expected of me with conventional jobs and relationships, even marrying my high school sweetheart, but *failed miserably* because I was so unfulfilled. I loved being in love, but mostly, I loved lust—resulting in numerous trysts, marriages and divorces. I eventually came to realize I was allergic to traditional family life and the drudgery of the establishment, so much so, I abandoned my family (two daughters and two sisters), friends, and acquaintances in my search for a higher quality of life. During my smuggling career, I kept in touch with none of my family, making new acquaintances as my career progressed.

At the onset of my smuggling career, which was Mexican marijuana into Southern California, I was in between relationships and almost all of my associates were related to the drug business. Providing a much needed reliable service to this culture—I was held in high esteem never afforded me in any of my previous occupations. I enjoyed this respect and the ease that I could now support myself.

Discovering the pleasures of smoking pot led to the introduction to those who had the best, which eventually were the importers, at that time, from Mexico into Southern California. When they discovered that I had special skills as a pilot, I was propositioned and enticed with a sum of $20K for a short one day trip to fly a load of kilos to a dry lake in the Mohave Desert where we were met by a ground crew to pick up the load.

The importer that hired me flew with me as I was unfamiliar with the operation. He directed me to a ranch about one hundred and fifty miles into Mexico. The owner had connections with the Federales and was allowed to maintain a dirt runway on the ranch where we were protected and allowed to land and depart as we pleased. The rancher also provided clean aviation gas for my Cessna 182 aircraft.

Everything went like clockwork until we were returning in the early afternoon, and as we approached the border near Nogales I became extremely paranoid. My mind ran rampant with visions of being tracked on radar; fearing it would be only moments before we were intercepted by military aircraft that had been scrambled from any number of air bases in the vicinity.

I reduced my altitude to fly through small canyons hoping to get below the imagined radar, all the time the importer assuring me that there was nothing to fear, having made this trip many times with other pilots. Once we got well into Southern California without being spotted and chased down, I regained my composure and completed the trip without any misfortune.

I declined a few more trips until I met an old experienced smuggler who invited me to accompany him on one of his trips deep into Baja Mexico. He assured me that my paranoia was normal and was a result of believing too many myths about the capabilities of the government catching smugglers. He rationalized all of the myths and disproved the theories by flying across the border at high noon at ten thousand feet over the city of San Diego like he had never left the air space of the U.S. Once I had seen how it was done by a pro, my services were again available and I retired from the establishment rat race.

I became involved in a relationship during this time and my lover was a career person; our relationship was more co-habitation than friendly. When the sex became monotonous, so did the relationship. That's when I read a book about personal liberty, said good-bye to my lover and decided to become an expatriate.

This would lead me to Sheldon and an ensuing new career as an international highflying cocaine smuggler.

CHAPTER SEVEN

TURNING POINT

BACK IN CALIFORNIA and living with Sheldon, I looked up Stringbean. He was pleased to hear from me. Since I had last seen him in Park City, he made a connection with a Colombian who was in the cocaine business. Stringbean had completed a few drug runs for him through various islands in the Caribbean. He told me that his connection was looking for a good twin engine airplane to purchase. It had to be suitable for the rigors of smuggling—which required special attributes not found in all aircraft. Stringbean had accepted this assignment and asked if I would be interested in locating this exceptional plane knowing that I had considerable knowledge about such things. I jumped at the opportunity, and Stringbean paid me a sizeable advance knowing the project was in good hands.

Sheldon and I upgraded our lifestyle. We moved to the beach area in Orange County while I conducted my search for the ideal plane. Life was looking much rosier indeed!

During this period, Stringbean was organizing a group of acquaintances to become pilots. It was his intention to supply the Colombians with accomplished smuggling pilots. These particular types of pilots are scarce due to attrition—the unqualified being dropped, arrested, or disappearing inroute; the professionals retiring early, usually because of wealth and common sense. I had the occasion to meet most of these recruits. Rob, from Park City, was one of them. Russ, from Southern California, was another. As a lure in recruiting pilots, Stringbean arranged elaborate meetings to socialize with these chaps in exotic clandestine settings; at times delivering us in a chartered Learjet to our destination.

I found a plane that met Stringbean's criterion. It was at the Orange County airport hangar in Southern California. It was a Piper Navajo—a strong, twin engine six passenger plane that had been maintained in immaculate condition by the corporate pilot who flew for the contractor owner. Stringbean liked it, and the Colombian was very pleased. He promptly sent the money to purchase it. Stringbean asked me to personally deliver the plane if I was interested. A sizable bonus was an inducement. He didn't know yet exactly where—but an island in the Caribbean was its destination. I was asked to fly the plane to Florida—to any place of my choice there—then call Stringbean and let him know my location. Whenever he received further instructions from the Colombian, he would contact me. In the meantime, I was to sit tight and enjoy myself. I chose Naples, a city on the Gulf Coast, as our destination; it being a bit quieter and slower than the fast paced resort areas on Florida's East Coast. Stringbean asked me to take Russ and his girlfriend along for the flying experience. I agreed, not expecting to be gone for more than a month. I had no trouble talking Sheldon into coming along on this little adventure.

We had been in Naples for a week or so, when Stringbean called and told me that our destination was an out island in the Bahamas called "Norman's Cay". I was asked to fly the plane there, check into the small hotel, and wait for the Colombian to show up. After turning the plane over to him, we were to stay on the island and enjoy ourselves until Stringbean arrived.

***

At this point, my life would change dramatically. Getting to this juncture had been quite a process—a combination of factors that led me from my all-American Pat Boone roots to the renegade life of a maverick entrepreneur. There were a few major turning points that landed me here.

First of all, I was unhappy. It was difficult for me to accept spending so much of my time chasing the buck in order to survive—doing something that I didn't enjoy. It was also difficult to maintain conventional relationships. I flitted from one relationship to another—hoping that the next would have some longevity—that the honeymoon would continue forever. Alas! That was never to be found by living in society. In retrospect, I can see clearly that my relationships were primarily motivated by LUST—which I mistook for love. Familiarity depletes the mental fantasy required to preserve the exhilaration previously experienced, thus dulls the excitement of lust and is compounded by the rigorous demands from living in society.

The first turning point in my melancholy lifestyle was when I was introduced to marijuana. This brought a feeling of much desired good cheer into my life. The pursuit of this exhilaration led me deep into the culture of this much used drug—eventually providing me with an alternative—earning a very good living-leaving me with much leisure time and utilizing a skill that I enjoyed. That's when I became a marijuana smuggler. I pursued this new career for several years without ever being discovered by law enforcement. However, I was still surviving in society and paying many of the same old dues-including failed relationships.

My second turning point occurred when a friend gave me a book—assuring that it would give me the solutions to the problems that I endured. Not being much of a reader, I reluctantly read it and it did indeed provide me with information that *changed my life forever.*

This was a handbook for personal liberty—outlining ways to live without being bound by social restrictions, family problems, etc. in order to be free to make one's own decisions. It explained the problems or "traps" found living in the establishment and logical solutions for dealing with them.

I was so taken by this wisdom that I ended a failing relationship and packed up my personal belongings. That's when I moved from Southern California to Park City, and it was there that my third turning point unfolded-taking a serious fancy to Sheldon. While I had been attracted to her before, during my limited visits at her mom's house, our relationship would now move on to a whole new level. As previously mentioned, her mother had followed me to Park City, bringing her cute young daughter with her. After months of fun in the snow, the time came to depart the now deserted resort and return to my source of income (smuggling pot out of Mexico into Southern California)—having depleted most of my savings. Sheldon was invited to come along with me.

That's when Sheldon's mom went to the local cops, lying that I had kidnapped Sheldon at gun point. THIS experience was my third turning point. I was languishing in the Salt

Lake county jail—awaiting my trial in Park City—expecting a sentence of at least thirty years for a kidnapping charge. I was so depressed at this point—I contemplated doing myself in. It was only weeks later I was free. This was significant because when I discovered the TRUTH of how the justice system really works—it became obvious that a person like me was in grave danger pressing my luck with the establishment in this country. Returning eventually to Southern California where my connections were, I was looking for a way to leave this war zone (USA) and become an expatriate. That's when, while living with Sheldon, I got the opportunity to purchase and deliver Piper Navajo N50RK to the Colombian at Norman's Cay.

CHAPTER EIGHT

NORMAN'S CAY

I OVERFLEW NORMAN'S CAY to get the lay of the land; this, after checking in to the Bahamas in Nassau, on the island of New Providence. After clearing customs at the airport of entry there, we were issued tourist permits for ninety days. We then refueled and departed for Norman's Cay—which is located in an archipelago known as the Exumas—some forty-four miles southeast of Nassau. South Florida is located approximately two hundred and ten miles away.

The first thing I noticed about flying low over the Bahamian islands is the abundant brilliant white sandy beaches. The water is as transparent as glass, making it possible to clearly see the bottom fifty feet deep, until the various shades of turquoise gradually turned into dark blue. There was very little dirt on most of the cays to contaminate the surrounding sea. There are no mountains on these cays—being the remnants of coral reefs formed millennia ago when the area was covered by water. The highest point on Norman's Cay was fifty feet above sea level. This is where the restaurant and bar were located—taking full advantage of the superb view. With very little soil on the island, the vegetation was sparse. It was limited to low bushes, coconuts, mangroves, and a few Austrian pines—all of which were able to tolerate the tropical heat, salt spray, and violent hurricanes with torrential rains.

Norman's looked like Paradise as we taxied off the paved three-thousand foot runway that sat on the southernmost tip of the island. After securing the plane, we walked the eighth mile to the small hotel; the modest tourist office at the airport being closed. There we found a few of the Bahamian staff and a couple of Americans that seemed to be in charge. It turned out that we were the only tourists on the island, and had our pick of the half dozen bungalows that lined a "Club Med" type beach.

After doing the tourist routine of hopping into our swimsuits and testing the clear warm water at our front door, we showered and had dinner, joining a few of the staff in the restaurant for some delicious homemade Bahamian cooking. We then turned in early, having had a very busy and different type of day.

CHAPTER NINE

AN ISLAND SCANDALOUS NAME

THERE'S SOME INTRIGUING history associated with Norman's Cay. In the days of the Spanish Main, many of the islands in the Bahamas were inhabited by various "Pirates of the Caribbean". This was to facilitate the fairly easy ambush of treasure laden Spanish galleons slogging their way northward from the plundering of Central and South America. The most recognized and notorious pirate at that time based his operation in what is now known as Nassau. He was Edward Teach—more commonly known as "Blackbeard". An associate, possibly an officer in Blackbeard's armada, occupied another island further east. His name was "Norman", thus as folklore has it, the island became known as Norman's Island or Norman's Cay. Naturally, rumors abound by the locals of the vast treasures that are hidden in secret caves on the island.

This, and many other islands in the Bahamas, has a reputation of being used throughout history as a way point for smuggling due to its close proximity to the United States. Not only are drugs being smuggled today, but whiskey during Prohibition, and just about anything else that was illegal in the United States.

The Norman's Cay part of my adventure that I am about to relate has been written about in books and magazine articles, and has been portrayed on television and in movies alike. I, myself, have been approached on many occasions, having been a part of this infamous story. I have declined all offers.

Actually, the true story is rather tepid—lacking much of the sex and violence that other authors have found necessary to include in their stories. Leave that as it may, my purpose for writing this story is to relive the memories that I experienced many years ago. If no other person reads what I have set down, it matters little to me—for I have achieved my purpose.

CHAPTER TEN

THE COLOMBIAN

NORMAN'S CAY IS about six miles long, and a tad over a quarter mile at its widest point. You could throw a rock across its narrowest. It contains about seven miles of what was once paved road. The roads, yacht club/hotel, marina, small convenience store, and a few other odds and ends were built by a resort development company many years ago. It is my understanding that the runway was built for emergency purposes by the United States during the Bay of Pigs incident; this prior to the development company purchasing the island. The company sub-divided most of the island, with the expectation of flying in potential customers, wining and dining them—and selling off beach front lots. There were a few lots sold, and a few vacation residences built—about a dozen in all as I recall. The company eventually failed and filed bankruptcy. The island and its assets reverted back to the financial company that had funded the project.

Most of the residences are located along the north end of the island. There is another dock and small marina located there, which is referred to as the pond—which, in fact, is a rather large and sheltered lagoon. There are a few slips there, and a couple of dilapidated boats encrusted with barnacles and dense moss growing on the neglected hulls.

Except for about a month every year, there are two large house boats moored in the pond. These belong to an affluent family that has them towed to other nearby islands to vacation on. A narrow channel at the extreme north end of Norman's separates it from a very small island called "Saddle Cay". One residence, made of stone, occupies this tiny island, and like most of the residences, is seldom occupied.

The nearest inhabited island is Highbourne Cay. It is three islands north of Norman's—a distance of no more than five miles as the pelican flies. Not having its own runway, it has permission to utilize Norman's, shuttling their passengers between the islands by boat.

When we arrived at the now defunct Norman's Cay, the only staff besides the Bahamians consisted of two Americans—one with his family. They were hired by the finance company that had repossessed the island, to protect the interests of the company until it could be disposed of. For all practical purposes, Norman's Cay was closed—except for the small Bahamian staff remaining there doing maintenance work.

It was quite some time before the Colombian showed up. While we were waiting, we explored the island and discovered some rental bungalows that were located on the west beach next to the runway. They were privately owned by a realtor who lived in south Florida. These villas had kitchenettes and were considerably more spacious than the hotel accommodations. The owner was anxious to generate a little income, and we struck a deal.

When the Colombian finally arrived, we discovered him to be a fit, tan and handsome lad of about thirty. Charismatic and charming, he had an outgoing personality. We immediately hit it off well. He informed us of his real name (Carlos Enrique Lehder Rivas) and we agreed on the name "Morgan" for business purposes and personal communication. I would be referred to as "Buccaneer". His intention was to stay on the island for a while, and he asked if we would remain there with him so that we could become better acquainted.

We talked a great deal about many things. Stringbean had filled me in on Morgan's background as a Colombian drug dealer, and Morgan had been informed of my expertise. He explained the difficulty of smuggling drugs into the United States by plane due to the limited range of small aircraft. Morgan knew the Colombians had a great need for a stop-over enroute, where a plane could land in "friendly" territory to refuel then continue its journey with enough range to be selective in its destination. He had scouted the Caribbean and discovered that Norman's Cay met the criterion required. Morgan had intentions of purchasing property on the island, similar to another group that lived in Florida and owned a residence and support equipment on Norman's Cay. They were in the pot smuggling business and had been doing it successfully for years.

There were other smaller operations using the island as well. Some landed and stashed fuel for the return trip to the states. This was usually hidden in the bushes around the airport. Others flew their drugs to the island and off-loaded their contraband to a boat moored at the marina, which completed the remainder of the trip. Norman's Cay was ideal for these types of operations due to being closed to tourism and no security on the island.

As a newly found friend, Morgan asked me stay on indefinitely, and become his personal pilot. In fact, I was the only pilot when Morgan and I first settled on Norman's Cay. Later on, after we became organized and I retired from the business, there would be many others that flew for Morgan's operation; a steady stream of drug runners that would come and go over time—as is the nature of pilots in this business due to becoming very wealthy in a short period of time. While Morgan and I would become exceptionally close friends, I was never his advisor (as prosecutors would later allege in our infamous trial) nor was I involved with his business activities except as the original pilot in our delivery system. In addition to smuggling, my other duties included flying to Nassau for shopping trips and hauling supplies.

Because of the failure of the resort company, most of the residences on the island were not occupied—except for rare short vacations by a few that didn't mind flying in their own supplies. This was a very expensive prospect indeed! Consequently, when Morgan located the house he wanted to buy—the owner felt that he had received a windfall—and was willing to negotiate almost any kind of deal. Not being the type to take advantage of a person's misfortune, Morgan paid fair market value. When other owners discovered this gift from heaven, most of them contacted Morgan, hoping to be as fortunate as their neighbor. Eventually, Morgan did purchase most of these properties, needing housing for his staff and security personnel.

There were four property owners that did not want to sell. One was the group from Florida that was smuggling pot. Another was a family from Boston. They had vacationed on the island when it was still primitive. The patriarch of this family was usually the only one that visited, staying for many months at a time. He was a fine old gentleman with many renowned friends that would visit him when he was on the island. Another elderly man owned a beach home on the island. He spent half of the year on Norman's, and the other half at Martha's Vineyard. Yet another home owner, who was a young entrepreneur, rarely visited the island—and when he did—seldom stayed more than a week or two at his lovely beach house. He was a pilot and was thought to be a promoter in the music business.

When Sheldon and I decided that we were going to stay on the island, Morgan loaned me the money to purchase a beach cottage from a family in the states. It was being occupied by one of the Americans working for the finance company. He had been the dive master for the defunct resort company.

During the time that we lived on the island, we turned this vacation cottage, which we named "Manazales", (most of the houses on the island had names), into a very comfortable and attractive home. All of the residences on the island had their own generators, and huge cisterns for holding rain water. We used propane for cooking, and our island communication system was VHF radio. Morgan had purchased an old Chesapeake Bay oyster fishing boat, the "Margaret Lee"—about sixty feet in length—that brought in most of the supplies. Fuel was delivered by barge from Nassau, and stored in large tanks at the marina. We had fuel and water delivery trucks for servicing the residences. There was one fresh water well that was for emergency purposes during a prolonged drought. Long leisurely showers were discouraged to our guests.

There came a time when Morgan was contacted by the finance company that owned the island. They offered him a deal that he couldn't refuse. Morgan ended up owning all of the property and assets on the island, except for those previously mentioned that were privately owned. When this occurred, Morgan set about restoring the island into an operational private resort. Morgan and I often discussed his ideas of offering choice properties to celebrities in the music business, as a beautiful and secure place to relax and play. One of the first major projects was to have two hangars built at the airport. These were large enough to accommodate medium sized business jets.

During this time, the island was being utilized for its intended purpose: a trans-shipment center for smuggling cocaine. Unless you knew what was going on—it would have been most difficult to detect.

"For whatever its worth, I can say with pride that I have never lost a load or been caught in the act of smuggling. I'm in prison for having been told on by associates that had been caught—the most dangerous part of any illegal enterprise." -JCR

CHAPTER ELEVEN

GETTING DOWN TO BUSINESS

"Excuse me, while I kiss the sky"—*Jimi Hendrix*

THE BASIC PROCEDURES for the operation of the business included three main functions of specialists: manufacturers, transportation and distribution. The groups involved in this scheme seldom deviated from their specialty due to their astute business practices. Our specialty was transportation. Thus, the stories the media reported and the testimony under oath about our Norman's Cay operation being involved in the distribution business—except for a few rare occasions for friends—are a misnomer by journalists and perjury by witnesses for perks by the government. Such misinformation may have contributed to the bogus stories of violence on Norman's Cay. This is not to say that there wasn't violence connected with the distribution business—as is almost always the case—but it had nothing to do with the transportation functions we were involved with.

The cocaine enroute was seldom on the island more than a couple of days,and during the peak of our tenure there, shipments averaged about two a month—(not like arrivals at LAX as some have speculated). The average shipment was in the neighborhood of two-hundred-and-fifty to three hundred kilos (not the tons that had been reported), largely determined by the weight and balance requirements, limitations, and restrictions of the aircraft we used.

The following is a typical example of how I, as a drug smuggling pilot, earned my keep using my special skills. A few prerequisites must be considered before undertaking this career. A pilot should have enough experience to be qualified as a "Bush" pilot—having to deal with a plethora of unexpected circumstances associated with the clandestine business of smuggling. This experience would include the ability to select the proper equipment to do the job safely and efficiently. Because of the stealthy nature of my career—I had to learn many new flying skills seldom encountered by the procedurally oriented pilots that have no inclination for entrepreneurship. A very important consideration is to have the ability to overcome the dreadful fear produced by paranoia. This is a must and I have seen highly qualified pilots freak out as the shore of the U.S. looms up on the horizon.

Thus, for a typical working flight on Norman's Cay, I preflight my strong and reliable twin engine Piper Navajo the day before my intended flight to Colombia-,which is a distance of approximately one thousand miles to the nearest landfall which would be the peninsula of La Guajira. In the baggage compartment, I will have stashed a folded thirty-five gallon rubber fuel bladder to be installed in the cabin over the wing and quickly coupled to the plane's regular fuel system. This will be filled with fuel at our destination along with the plane's normal capacity, which has a range of about nine hundred miles on economy cruise.

Morgan will fly with me on these trips and be the negotiator on Colombian soil. We also carry aboard the plane an emergency locator transmitter and a compact four man life raft for the long trip over the Caribbean after passing over the island of Hispaniola. A direct flight from Norman's Cay would take us directly over Cuba, which we avoid out of courtesy to Mr. Castro and our own safety.

After departing Norman's Cay early, we set a course for Turks and Caicos Islands, a few hundred miles south, where we will top off the plane's regular fuel tanks. Not having any contraband aboard, this is a safe straight forward procedure. We can't do this on the return trip; thus the reason for the extra thirty-five gallons in the bladder. With the fuel stop, this is about a six hour trip to our destination under normal weather conditions. At this time in history there was no GPS available (not for civilian use) and the long trip over the Caribbean was done by dead reckoning (calculating and tracking a proper wind correction heading to stay on course, referencing periodic fixes or visual landmarks if any), which will keep you up on the wheel for what seems like an eternity.

As we approach Colombia, we will pick up a VOR (VHF omnidirectional range is a radio navigation aid for aircraft) on one of the Netherland Antilles ABC Islands, and make any necessary heading correction for our destination and calculate our fuel remaining, now that we have the VOR to verify our position and course by. Only on rare occasion did Carlos use the same landing strip where the cargo and fuel were shuttled in by Colombian pilots and stashed. Consequently, almost each trip was a new challenge, and being in the middle of the desert you could depend on good weather and dirt runways, with erosion having taken its toll—leaving washouts, ruts, holes—and plenty of various sized rocks. These makeshift runways were usually of sufficient length, but each was a challenging obstacle course to maneuver through on take-off and landing.

On a pre-arranged radio communication frequency, as I overflew the strip enough times to select the safest landing area, Morgan would contact his ground crew and have them light a small fire so I could determine wind direction. After landing, I would service the plane and refuel, using a funnel and chamois to capture debris and water in the fuel that came out of questionable containers. The cargo wasn't loaded until the plane was ready to leave early the next morning. Sometimes the plane was covered with a camouflage net to reduce its exposure to any overflying aircraft. While it was still daylight, I would walk the full length of the runway, pitching off rocks and memorizing the best path to take the following morning.

Most of the runways in this area of Colombia had some type of bulldozer. The first time I noticed one, I asked Morgan if its purpose was to keep the runway in condition. He revealed that it was seldom used for that purpose—its main function was to remove any plane blocking the runway and disposing of it if it was unable to depart under its own power. If a plane was disabled for whatever reason and couldn't be repaired within a few hours, the bulldozer would dig out a pit, drain any fuel in the plane, crush it into a compact mass—push it in the pit, and bury it. This action was to deter Federales from coming into the area to conduct investigations.

Morgan told me a story about losing an Aero Commander to the pit on one of these runways. The pilot was rolling out on take-off and ran the nose wheel into a deep rut—tearing it off—with the plane coming to a screeching halt. After unloading the cargo and several passengers, the plane was disposed of, much to the chagrin of Morgan, who now had to not only regroup but had the responsibility of a grounded pilot on his hands.

Eating and sleeping facilities at these remote runways were pretty Spartan-, a bed usually being a hammock strung between some posts in a make-shift hut. Security personnel roamed the area all night long, ensuring that nothing happened to the plane, cargo, and crew. None of this was conducive to a good night's rest, and just before sunrise, per my request—I was awakened to have some breakfast, supervise the loading of our cargo, and walk the runway one last time before take-off. I never departed until there was enough light to see the runway and its obstructions clearly.

After take-off and climbing to altitude, it was only a short time before the beautiful Caribbean came into view, and I turned over the flying to the autopilot while Carlos and I monitored the systems and chatted for the next five or so hours.

Arrival at Norman's Cay was casual—being in home territory. Our ground security was contacted and I overflew the island making sure there were no strange boats or planes that couldn't be accounted for. We had an alternate island we could fly to if there was any problem on Norman's. The plane was hangared; the cargo unloaded, and placed in a secure cave until it was time for the trip to the states.

If I were flying that leg, it would usually be to one of three different locations in the middle of Florida; one on a dirt country road, and the other two in cow pastures on isolated ranches. For this trip I needed a strong reliable plane with rough and short field capabilities. I used a C-206, which did the job well. Known as the Cessna Stationair, this six seat single-engine fixed gear aircraft boasts a powerful engine, rugged construction, and a large cabin which makes it a popular bush plane—perfect for my particular needs. This fairly short leg of the trip didn't require any elaborate fuel planning.

Early morning departure from Norman's Cay was the norm, and after lift-off, I would take a heading for Freeport on the island of Grand Bahama—a distance of about two hundred miles. Simulating an approach to a small airport on the west end of the island, I would change my heading due west and maintain a low altitude of about one hundred feet over the Gulf Stream for the sixty mile trip to West Palm Beach Florida. About a mile offshore, I would perform a tight 360 degree turn to make sure I wasn't being tailed—and take a heading north, paralleling the coast below the skyline of the towering hotels along the beach. This, of course, was to help elude any radar from the many airports in this area. After several miles, I would then climb to a thousand feet and head inland for the last fifty miles of my journey.

On a seldom used frequency, I would contact my ground pick-up crew and overfly my landing area, making sure no other vehicles were nearby, and make my landing—at times in pasture that was two feet high—requiring extra attention.

After a few minutes of unloading, I was back in the air, with a quick fuel stop at a small airport and heading directly back to the island-, outdistancing the build-up of afternoon cumulonimbus clouds prevalent in South Florida.

Back on Norman's Cay, after securing my trusty 206, I would chat with Morgan for a while about the trip and head for my cozy home and my much missed companions—Sheldon and Norman. Within a week I would have another substantial deposit in my bank account.

To justify my covert activities, I rationalized that smuggling drugs was not a real crime, an infringement on the life, liberty or pursuit of my fellow man's happiness. If the manufacturing and selling of alcohol and tobacco were considered legal by the minds in Washington-, I surmised that the drugs that I supplied should be legal also and the only reason they were not was due to another self-gratifying scheme by a corrupt government; therefore, I considered myself not a renegade but an entrepreneur—with a potential risk of being punished for violating a mandate—not a crime against humanity. I was respected, well paid, and enjoyed the challenge of out-smarting the so-called 'invincible'.

I made the mistake of not knowing that I could be punished for another person's actions, and hearsay evidence-, falsely assuming that I had to be caught in the act of actually breaking the law—which I never was.

For whatever its worth, I can say with pride that I have never lost a load or been caught in the act of smuggling. I'm in prison for having been told on by associates that had been caught—the most dangerous part of any illegal enterprise.

Once that I discovered how inept the law enforcement agencies were in real life and not the fiction that they spoon feed the public, the risk factor of getting caught diminished considerably—taking necessary precautions, of course, and not being blatantly complacent about the government's existence. The risk of getting caught was slim to none-,the exception being through infiltration by a snitch.

Because our operation was extremely well organized and low profile, Sheldon was aware—but basically oblivious—to our business activities, and spent her time being an 'island girl' and enjoying a high quality of life. She was pampered and spoiled rotten. I assured her I would always take care of her, and that she would never have to work or worry about the almighty buck.

Sheldon was content with our adventurous and carefree lifestyle. She never expressed any concern about being caught and arrested.

My true role in the island operation bore little semblance to the "Kingpin" status prosecutors would later allege it to be.

I was really nothing more than a very close friend of Morgan's and a professional drug smuggler as a pilot, who only worked long enough to help establish the business. When I was not engaged in drug runs or other pilot duties, and when it was necessary for Morgan to leave the island to take care of business elsewhere, I would oversee the island's maintenance.

CHAPTER TWELVE

COCAINE

THE LURE OF any smuggling operation is fueled by the insane amount of dollars it generates. Our island operation was no exception. The money grew on trees (so to speak), with its roots in rural Colombia. The following is the basic concept of the farmer to market procedure; and the distribution of the money:

The business starts with the farmers in South America growing the coca plant—a perennial shrub that is partially stripped of its leaves—and through a simple inexpensive procedure-,the leaves are reduced to the basic ingredients needed to produce cocaine through further processing. This product is called Bazuco (base) in Colombia. At the time that we were in business, the farmers received five hundred dollars for a kilo of this product. It was purchased by dealers like Pablo (Escobar) and sent to their labs for the final processing, using expensive and illegal chemicals like ether and acetone. This process would cost about another five thousand dollars per kilo.

Now the cocaine would have to be shipped safely to the market—the United States—and that's the service that we provided (transportation) for any dealer that wanted to pay our fee of five thousand dollars per kilo to deliver it to their agent in the U.S.

At that time, a kilo of coke purchased in the Southeastern U.S. would cost no less than fifty thousand dollars. After expenses, the dealer and his group of distributors would net approximately forty thousand dollars per kilo. If the load consisted of two hundred kilos (four hundred and forty pounds), the dealer would net approximately eight million dollars. Morgan would be paid one million for arranging the transportation, and the pilot would receive two hundred and fifty thousand dollars from Morgan if he flew both legs of the trip, from Colombia to Norman's Cay, and then from Norman's to the states.

CHAPTER THIRTEEN

ISLAND LIFE

DURING THE ISLAND'S peak operation, there were about thirty-five employees living there. A third consisted of Bahamians doing island maintenance. The rest were Colombians—men and women—handpicked to take care of the efficient operation of the island. This included a team of trained security personnel that patrolled 24/7. They were headed up by a lad who took his job very seriously, and he did it very well.

Because the business part of the island's operation was of little consequence, and for the most part ran quite smoothly, it was pretty much without incident; even though incredible stories about it have made the media, obviously from people with very vivid imaginations. Norman's Cay was a peaceful little paradise with much socializing. There were BBQ's, kite flying, skin and scuba diving, parasailing, and island hopping by boat and plane. Island fun stuff!

My typical day on Norman's was an early rise, with a hearty breakfast cooked on my commercial Wolf range in my beach bungalow. I had a VW Thing which I would take on a tour of the island, sometimes with Sheldon, always with Norman. I'd stop by Morgan's hacienda (we were next door neighbors on the beachfront) for a cup of real Colombian coffee, some Colombian smoke and Colombian camaraderie. About once a week I would fly a couple of the cooks to Nassau for some shopping. Every few weeks I would make a trip to Colombia for business purposes (drug runs) in N50RK, my dependable Piper Navajo. Most of my time was spent with my family—Sheldon and Norman—at home, and servicing my generators and fresh water system. We had a canoe for trips to nearby Saddle Cay, and frequently visited isolated beaches for picnics and snorkeling. We had access to all of Morgan's toys, but seldom used them, being content with simpler pleasures and each other's company.

So, overall, island life was pretty peaceful with few exceptions. There were a couple of incidents where Morgan had to intervene to keep his high-strung head of security, who was overzealous at times, from harshly dealing with people on the island who had made some bad judgments. One such incident involved a lad who had secretly started his own little smuggling venture, arranging for a friend to land his float plane in the pond to pick up some drugs. This lad lived aboard his boat, which was moored in the pond. When Morgan got word of this, he simply paid him for his boat, and had one of his pilots deliver him to Florida, with the request that he not return to Norman's. Morgan detested violence and would not tolerate it or hard drug use among his staff on the island. There was always as much good Colombian pot as you wanted to smoke.

Morgan purchased a large luxury yacht, which at one time had belonged to the Shah of Iran during his stay in the Bahamas. Morgan contracted with the island resident from Martha's Vineyard to take his yacht to Florida for some modifications. After many months and a great deal of expense, Morgan requested that the yacht be returned to the island. With much anxiety, the resident complied, after loading his own piano aboard the yacht. He and a skipper he hired came directly to Norman's Cay without checking in through customs. Upon its arrival, we all met it at the dock, eager to see the modifications. Alas! In a moment, it was quite obvious that nothing had been done, and to add insult to injury, the boat had been trashed. To say the least, Morgan was not too happy to see his once beautiful yacht reduced to resembling a garbage scow. Without conversation, Morgan sent his security people to have a talk with this stupid scoundrel. He was advised that it would be in his best interest to leave the island immediately, which he did. He went straight to customs in Nassau, where he reported that Morgan had brought his yacht into the Bahamas illegally without clearing customs. Shortly thereafter, the Bahamian Police showed-up, confiscated the yacht, and without an experienced skipper aboard, ran across a reef while leaving the pond, holing it. This was a sizable financial loss for Morgan, and possibly for the negligent resident. He returned on one occasion—sneaking on the island with two police escorting him, which was allowed by the island security. He was to discover that his home had been vandalized.

There came a time when the Florida pot smuggling organization on the island discovered they could make more money flying cocaine than pot, so they joined forces with the Colombians. Morgan furnished them with an airplane—a Merlin Turboprop—similar to the one that transported Sheldon and me from Panama to the States. They discovered through their connections in Florida that they had been indicted for their pot smuggling venture. They decided that to keep from being arrested, they would load their families and crew aboard their two old planes and move—lock, stock, and barrel—to Norman's Cay. The DEA soon discovered their whereabouts. They had no jurisdiction in the Bahamas, yet were always lurking nearby.

The agents cruised around the island in an old yacht, disguised to look like a Bahamian fishing boat. It had what appeared to be several high tech antennas attached to it. It was rather obvious that the boat didn't belong to a poor Bahamian. There was an attempt to swim ashore from a boat anchored off shore, with the agents met by the island security. They even landed on the island in a twin-engine plane, posing to be doctors on a fishing vacation. Security surrounded the plane and sent word to Morgan, who just happened to have a Bahamian immigration officer on the island as a guest. The officer asked to see their immigration entry permits, which they didn't have. Their personal identification revealed they were DEA agents, with no written authority to be in the Bahamas. He reprimanded them for being in the country illegally, and instead of escorting them back to Nassau, advised them to return directly to the United States. A full report of this violation, directed to Washington, would be forthcoming. They then convinced our neighbors at Highbourne Cay that they should be allowed to set up headquarters on their island to monitor our radio communications and activities. We were informed of this plot, and a message was sent requesting a meeting with the manager of Highbourne. He was advised that as long as he continued to violate our neighborly alliance, our airport was no longer at his disposal. The DEA packed up and left.

An unfortunate side effect of this development was the discovery by the DEA of our Colombian cocaine operation, which to our knowledge, was unknown before the group from Florida permanently moved to the island. The U.S. government pressed Bahamian authorities to take action against the Norman's Cay operation. It wasn't long before raids were being conducted on the island. Having connections in the Bahamian government, we were always well advised of these impending raids. Consequently, nothing of any importance was ever discovered. The raids proved to be an inconvenience, not only for us, but for the police as well. It required increased security on the island, because of the ever lurking DEA. They attempted to send ex-island residents to infiltrate the organization. They were welcome to visit the island, as was anyone that wanted to stop by, or needed some type of assistance. There were just certain areas that were off limits to visitors. The island and its facilities were available to anyone except antagonists to the island's function.

Even though this was Morgan's policy, the island—through the grapevine—quickly gained a notorious reputation. Media reports of boats supposedly discovered drifting offshore—with the slain bodies of the cruisers whose vessels had ventured too close to Norman's—were preposterous. No way was there ever a need for such violence. Common sense dictates it would have caused way too much heat and unwanted attention! Nevertheless, only the bravest souls would make use of the marina and airport. Most travelers in that part of the Bahamas gave Norman's Cay wide berth for fear of their very lives.

In reality, it appeared that the Bahamian government wasn't too interested in ridding their small country of a major source of income second only to the tourist business. They didn't have the resources to conduct expensive time consuming raids on islands, requiring transportation by boat or airplanes for those islands with runways.

Stepping out on my beachfront porch one morning, I was surprised to see a large Coast Guard vessel which appeared to be a cutter. It was sitting as close to the island as possible. The resident from Boston showed up at my place in his old World War II Jeep to have a better view of this situation. He pointed out that several of the large dish antennas aboard the vessel were pointed skyward. He theorized that the Coast Guard was establishing satellite co-ordinates, and that surveillance of Norman's was undoubtedly the object of this maneuver.

We had a high performance helicopter on the island which was a rarity in the Bahamas at the time. It's pilot was just returning from a trip to Nassau, and decided to check out this large ship. When the ship's crew saw the chopper coming, it secured everything in a matter of seconds. After flying around the ship, the chopper returned to the island, and the ship rapidly left the area.

CHAPTER FOURTEEN

THE ICONIC C-46

ANOTHER INTERESTING EVENT that occurred on the island evolved into a bit of an urban legend. It involved the arrival one afternoon of an old World War II aircraft. It was a C-46, a large twin-engine transport plane utilized to carry troops and cargo. It turned out that the pilot was an English man referred to as "British Andy". He had at one time done some flying for the organization. He discovered this old relic in Florida and found out that it was for sale. Thinking Morgan might be interested in buying it to haul cargo, he talked the owner into letting him fly it to Norman's Cay. Morgan wasn't interested, but invited Andy to spend a few days on the island.

Andy had a drinking problem, and had been known to take along a six-pack for company on many of his flights. Being on a short vacation seemed like a reasonable excuse for starting his favorite pastime first thing in the morning. One mid-morning, he decided to drop by the airport, being a bit tipsy, to fire-up the old sled and shoot some touch and goes, which is pilot language for practice take-offs and landings. He asked an unsuspecting

Colombian lad to join him in his venture and off they went. As Andy made his approach for the first landing, he miscalculated the beginning of the runway and touched down short. Realizing his error at the last moment, he gave the old girl full throttle to execute a go-around. To his great dismay, he clipped an earthen berm, tearing the left landing gear loose from its housing, leaving it dangling from the aircraft by cables and hoses. The plane then dipped low enough for the propeller on the left engine to strike the runway—bending it—and rendering it useless. With the right engine roaring and straining to keep the plane airborne, a bit of altitude was gained. It was only enough to clear the runway though, and make a slow settling arc to the left, running out of flying speed and altitude about a block offshore of the marina in front of the hotel. The plane belly-flopped to a splashing spectacular halt in shallow water, about half of it submerged.

Many of us witnessed this fiasco. A boat at the marina made a quick trip to the site of the crash and rescued the two survivors, neither one of whom had a scratch. Morgan furnished transportation for the embarrassed pilot back to the states. The plane has sat in this location for decades, deteriorating, and being slightly repositioned by passing hurricanes. Having become an iconic image of Norman's Cay over the years, it has been visited by countless snorkelers, curious boaters and relic collectors. Stories about its demise—the most popular tale being that the plane was too overloaded with kilos to fly, with its pilots high on coke—were created by the most vivid imaginations. Like most of the stories about the infamous Norman's Cay that I am aware of—only a few portray a semblance of the truth.

CHAPTER FIFTEEN

ON THE MOVE

ISLAND LIFE WASN'T like it used to be. With the potential threat to the island, uneasiness prevailed. Morgan sensed the threat of a possible attempt to kidnap him. Two men were recruited from Germany to be his personal body guards. Gone were the days of leisurely BBQ's on the beach and diving on the pristine reefs and adjoining islands. This—combined with the frequent raids disrupting our lifestyle—prompted Sheldon and me to consider taking a look at moving to another part of the world.

We considered British Columbia. With a reputation of being one of the most beautiful places on earth, this locale was fetching. After discussing our idea with Morgan, he agreed, knowing the island had lost its charm, and now only had value for conducting business. We took care of our affairs, and Morgan sent us on our way in one of his business jets. He promised he would be our first visitor if we liked Canada and decided to stay.

There were three passengers on this trip—Sheldon, myself, and Norman—the Golden Retriever I had purchased for Sheldon's birthday on one of my many trips to Florida. He was a cuddly puppy then, and had grown into a handsome seventy-five pound bundle of joy. He was our constant companion. After checking out of the Bahamas, we flew directly to Toronto where we spent the night. The next day, we completed the final leg of our trip flying across Canada to Calgary. The plane experienced a hydraulic malfunction, but our pilots made a safe and uneventful landing. With the plane being grounded until mechanics could be flown in to repair the system, Sheldon, Norman, and I bid the pilots farewell, and made the rest of the trip to British Colombia in a rental car.

We drove beautiful highways up and over the Rocky Mountains, with the postcard city of Banff located at the summit. The Rockies in this area are absolutely breathtaking—reminiscent of calendar pictures of the Swiss Alps; in fact, all of British Columbia was equally magnificent, consisting of one mountain range after another.

We eventually found an old mining community called Kimberly, located in one of the valleys. It was a charming little village maintaining a Bavarian motif. While searching for a permanent home, we rented a small condo at the local ski resort which was closed during the summer months.

With great determination, we finally found a cabin on the shore of a beautiful lake at the foot of the Rockies. It was twenty miles from Kimberly, and eight miles up a canyon gravel road. To get there, we had to pass through three ranches and an old mining ghost town with only a few structures remaining.

We settled into our new home, purchased a Bronco to negotiate rough winter terrain, ordered a couple cords of firewood, and fell into a relaxed mood once again. This was a completely different type of environment; one that we had never experienced before. Like the island, this was another unique lifestyle, much superior to "establishment" living.

At our cabin retreat, we provided drinking water, food treats and salt licks for the many deer that visited us during the winter months. Norman was hypnotized by them, sitting motionless on the porch watching their activities. During the winter, Norman's hair grew exceptionally thick, and on our morning walks in sub-freezing temperatures, ice cycles would hang from his slobbery lips. He missed his daily swim in the lake which was now frozen over, but never missed the opportunity to go ice fishing with me. He was a great pal and I loved him dearly.

We organized our wilderness cabin for maximum comfort. We invited friends to visit and share our new found paradise, as we had done on Norman's Cay. Several friends that we had known from Park City had been invited to the island before we departed. Dyan was one, who was our guest for several months. While on the island, she met one of Morgan's Colombian amigos, who was also vacationing. She was persuaded to accompany him back to Colombia for an indefinite stay

There was Steve from Montana, who had since married a red-headed "ski bunny" from Park City. Both of them visited and loved the island lifestyle. Morgan gave Steve a job and a place to live so that he and his wife could stay on the island.

Even Sheldon's Mom enjoyed a visit to Norman's Cay, the animosity once again forgotten. Sadly, consequences from that visit would one day play a major role in my incarceration. But at the time, these were pleasant visits for all concerned.

All had departed the island before we left for Canada. When we contacted Steve, who was back in Colorado, he and his wife dropped what they were doing and drove their Porsche up to visit us.

They loved British Columbia so much; they purchased a home near our place. We occasionally got together and socialized.

Ed, the organizer of the Florida pot smuggling group from Norman's, and his wife, also came to see us in Canada. Sheldon and I had become friends with them and their family. Their visit was in the dead of winter and we shared the new experience of riding snow machines on old mining and logging roads in the rugged mountains that surrounded the valley we lived in. We all enjoyed these times very much. At the time I couldn't have possibly imagined that one day, Ed, too, would play in a contributing role in locking me up for life.

I contacted Morgan and told him of our new location. We made arrangements for him to visit. We arrived at the airport at the predetermined time to pick him up. An unfamiliar Lear jet landed with Chuck, Morgan's jet and helicopter pilot at the controls, along with his co-pilot; but Morgan was not aboard the plane. He had been detained with business and sent Chuck up to persuade us to fly back to the island for our visit. We had commitments that precluded us from accepting his invitation. We invited the pilots to stay as our guests and rest for a few days at our cabin before heading back. They managed to squeeze in a couple of days with little convincing. They explained that Morgan's jet was in for maintenance, and the Lear they flew up was a leased plane to take up the slack. Oddly enough, it, too, had developed an engine problem on the way up and needed attention.

After departing Canada, the pilots flew to Florida and contacted Morgan who had an urgent trip that required them to fly a business associate to Colombia. Rather than take time to locate another plane, the pilots opted to nurse the troubled Lear for this important trip, with plans to put it in the shop when they returned.

This particular model of Lear jet didn't have the range to fly non-stop to its destination in Colombia, thus necessitating a fuel stop in Port-au-Prince, Haiti.

It was dark and overcast when the pilots contacted the Tower there, reporting sixty miles out. There was no indication of a problem.

Port-au-Prince sits in a valley surrounded by mountains. For a reason never determined, the plane got off course—positioned outside the mountain range—rather than inside the valley as prescribed in the normal approach procedure to the runway. The plane hit the side of a mountain, crashing into a small village, killing everyone onboard and several villagers.

When the U. S. government got word of the crash, they sent NTSB investigators to the scene, along with the DEA, thinking the plane was carrying a large sum of drug money to Colombia. Nothing was discovered that indicated any illegal activity. I have often wondered what circumstances would have prevailed had Sheldon and I accepted Morgan's invitation to return to the island in the ill-fated Lear.

CHAPTER SIXTEEN

SAVING NORMAN

WHEN WE FIRST arrived in Canada, we took Norman to the vet for a check-up. It was discovered that he had the first stages of heartworms, a life threatening situation over a period of time. Canada had a very low incidence of heart worm cases; the egg being carried by infested female mosquitoes. Consequently, there were no veterinarians in our area that were qualified to treat Norman; the cure requiring a delicate procedure needing a specialist to perform it. We located a vet in Saskatoon, Saskatchewan, who felt he could successfully administer the treatment. With great diligence, he made the attempt, but failed. In an effort to save Norman, and after much inquiry, the doctor located a renowned specialist at a University in Mississippi. Arrangements were made to have Norman treated there a few weeks later. Since we didn't know how long we would be gone, we left our cabin in the care of a friend in Kimberly.

Arriving in Mississippi, Sheldon and I took Norman to the University to meet the vet. He informed us that we could expect to be in town for at least a month. This personable young man arranged for us to rent a temporary apartment through a friend of his. He also helped us rent a safe deposit box with another friend who managed a local bank. I had brought along some valuables that needed safe keeping.

We checked Norman into the veterinary hospital where he was to remain under close observation for the full term of his treatment. We would be allowed to visit him only after the critical part of the treatment was finished; this, to prevent him from becoming overly excited. During our stay, we socialized with the doctor and his family and friends. We were treated exceptionally well by these hospitable people.

Once Norman's treatment was successfully completed, we decided that before heading back to Canada, we would all take a short vacation to Cozumel, a beautiful island off the east coast of Mexico. Since we were planning to bring Norman back to Mississippi in thirty days for a follow-up exam, I left some of my personal items in a blue suitcase with the doctor, and my valuables in the bank, having paid a year's rent on the safe deposit box. We called our friend Dyan in California and asked her to join us on our trip to Mexico. The four of us headed south on a chartered plane. We relaxed, did a few typical touristy things, and ate plenty of good food.

CHAPTER SEVENTEEN

COLOMBIAN CAMARADERIE

WHILE IN COZUMEL, I decided to give Morgan a call and see how my dear friend was doing on Norman's Cay. He was pleased to hear from us, and insisted that before we return to Mississippi, we stop by the island for a visit. He would have his jet in Cozumel the very next morning to pick us up.

We landed on Norman's Cay that afternoon, having over flown the island and discovering that a rainstorm had just passed—leaving the runway wet. Three thousand feet of wet runway is not sufficient to safely stop a Lear jet without thrust reversers. Our pilots flew to a nearby island with a dry runway where they dropped us off and proceeded on to Florida. Once there, one of the pilots flew his personal Beechcraft Bonanza, a single engine six seat high performance aircraft, back to pick us up and delivered us safely to our old home. It was great to see Morgan and other friends again.

The island hadn't changed much. A few new faces and business as usual. Morgan invited us to fly to Colombia with him for a short visit while he took care of some business there. Dyan was still with us, and we all boarded a different Lear jet, our destination being Cali. It was late when we arrived. We cleared customs and immigration and checked into a deluxe hotel.

We were advised late that night that our plane had been impounded by the Federales for investigation. Bribes had to be paid to the airport nightshift to allow us to take off before the dayshift came to work the next morning. Arriving at the airport with only minutes to spare, we ripped the confiscation tape from the jet's door, and literally threw our baggage in the plane as the pilots were starting the engines. The door was secured moments before full throttles were applied, and we accelerated down the runway. Some of the day crew, now in the Tower, ordered us to abort our takeoff. The pilots lifted off and rocketed to cruise altitude. Our course was due north, departing Colombia as quickly as possible.

Another Colombian trip afforded us more time to enjoy the region. Morgan had acquired a Sabreliner 60, a mid-sized business jet accommodating up to twelve passengers. He invited a few of his closest associates, including myself, to join him on a trip to Colombia in this newly acquired jet—a combination test flight and goodwill trip. He wanted to show us around his hometown of Armenia and introduce us to some of his friends. We also had plans to visit other cities in his beautiful country.

I was reluctant to be separated from Sheldon for over a week, having been almost constant companions for quite some time. But this was a man's trip, and to ask for an invitation for Sheldon to tag along would have been out of place. She encouraged me to go, which I did, but was sorry that she would miss the experience.

After departing Norman's Cay and refueling in Haiti, we entered Colombia through Bogota, the Capitol. None of us had visas, but Morgan had a unique system for cutting through the red tape by introducing the immigration officer to Benjamin Franklin. We stayed at one of the finest hotels, spent days taking in the highlights, and visited another old and interesting city—Barranquilla. We filed a flight plan for Armenia, our final destination. Upon landing at the airport, we learned that the aviation authorities there had not been notified of our flight plan and arrival. Because ours was the first jet to ever visit this small countryside airport, there was much confusion about procedure, and the Federales were notified to straighten things out. Morgan's charm paid off yet again, and we were free to proceed into town chauffeured by a caravan of Morgan's amigos from Armenia.

Road blocks, called "retens" are not uncommon in Colombia. They are attributed to the unrest between government and guerrilla factions in this country. You never know where and when a reten would be set up.

On this particular day, there happened to be one on the road we were traveling. No amount of charm, diplomacy, or bribery would work on these heavily armed lads. After a roadside interrogation, we were escorted into town to the local headquarters where we were informed that we were not being arrested, but rather, "detained". They weren't quite sure whether they had bad guys or possibly influential good guys. The fact that we arrived by private jet gave them cause to treat us with some respect, until their investigation and intervention by Morgan's attorney convinced them that we were indeed who we claimed to be. We were released, with apologies for the inconvenience. Afterwards, it wasn't too difficult to detect that our every move was being watched during our stay in town.

Morgan's hometown was picturesque at an elevation of over three thousand feet. Some of the finest coffee plantations are located here. We met some of Morgan's longtime friends, all gentlemen of the highest caliber who treated us royally. They had a school brotherhood that they referred to as "CCQ", an acronym for Cannabis Club of Quindío, an exclusive club named after their shared fondness for pot.

Our departure was without incident until we arrived back in Bogota to refuel. Immigration detained us at the airport for several hours while we were individually interrogated and strip searched. The officers went through the plane with a fine toothed comb, suspecting that we were carrying drugs. When they brought out the hand drill to bore search holes in our suitcases, one member of our group had had enough. He told them resentfully, with a few expletives, that they didn't have to go to the trouble of boring holes in his suitcase, and proceeded to rip out the linings. We were to discover at a later date that U.S. DEA agents—who had kept out of sight—had directed this harassment.

There was a sign of relief as we reached cruising altitude and once again saw the shores of Colombia appear, and the beautiful blue Caribbean come into view. Shortly, I would be back on Norman's Cay with my beloved Sheldon whom I had missed from the moment I left.

CHAPTER EIGHTEEN

MISSISSIPPI MISHAP

OUR STAY ON Norman's stretched on longer than anticipated. Rather than return to Mississippi for Norman's follow-up vet appointment, and then back to Canada, as previously planned, we settled back into our familiar and comfortable lives on the island.

We invited a couple of friends from Canada to visit us on Norman's. They were so overwhelmed by our lifestyle, they asked if they could stay. They were given a cottage and jobs making purchases for the island.

They were sent to the states to try to locate some rural property with a runway on it. I requested that at some point in their trip, when convenient, that they stop by Mississippi and contact the veterinarian that had treated Norman. They were to explain to him that Sheldon, Norman and I were back on the island indefinitely, and didn't know just when we would be back in the states. I asked them to request that he give them the personal property I had left in his care. When the couple returned to the island, I was told that the doctor had refused to give up the property without some type of authorization. Because they were the only people, beside Dyan, that knew that Sheldon and I had been in Mississippi, it is presumed that they were interrogated by the DEA upon entering or leaving the states. Apparently, they provided details about us, along with information about the island that only insiders would know.

At any rate, it was later discovered that the DEA made a trip to the doctor's town and informed the local police that a suspected drug dealer had visited there. This was big news in a town that could be likened to "Mayberry". The local sleuths gave their investigation special priority. Lacking sophisticated legal expertise and probable cause, they never-the-less confiscated our personal effects from the doctor, and subsequently discovered the safe deposit box where I had placed my valuables for safe keeping.

As if I were irresponsible enough to leave anything illegal in my personal effects, or in my safe deposit box, the local Sherlock's went on a search and managed to find a small stash of pot in my suitcase. They then went to a Justice of the Peace for a search warrant for my safety deposit box. He readily granted their request. The warrant stated that drugs were suspected of being in the box; however, nothing illegal was found. Some paperwork and cash assets were the only contents.

Based solely on what the DEA "suspected", and told the to the local investigators, they invented a case—and the District Attorney brought an indictment against my cash assets. No charges were brought against me personally.

I lost a sizeable amount of money when the courts took my assets to trial for being suspected proceeds from drug dealing. Because I couldn't be located to defend my assets, which were, in fact, proceeds from the sale of some property on the island

and which I could have proven given the opportunity—the court awarded the county my assets by default. The fact that the assets were in a paid-up safe deposit box—in my true name, and nothing illegal-—didn't seem to make any difference.

CHAPTER NINETEEN
THE HEAT IS ON

BACK ON NORMAN'S Cay, things were not going well between Morgan and the smuggling group from Florida that was seeking refuge on the island from the DEA. Personal differences between them had created deep-seated animosity that could not be resolved. Knowing that I had a friendly relationship with Ed, the head of the group (as previously mentioned, both he and his wife had visited Sheldon and me at our cabin in Canada), Morgan asked that I be an intermediary in resolving the conflict. At Morgan's request, I proposed a very generous offer from him to purchase all of the group's assets on the island-,the condition being that they had to pack up and leave. They turned a deaf ear to our proposal.

The hostility grew, and the island security convinced the group that it would be in their best interest to vacate the island immediately, which they did in their original pot smuggling planes.

The island once again resumed a semblance of tranquility. We later learned that Ed's group (smuggling crew and their families) had relocated to Haiti, where one can live in splendor on very little money. With that many people keeping in touch with the states, it didn't take long for the DEA to discover their new location. With the assistance of the Haitian police, the DEA set a trap for the group. It is rumored that the entire group was captured at the airport on some false pretense, whereupon they were promptly loaded into a vintage DC-3 and returned to their homeland.

The group was quite willing to divulge details regarding Morgan and the island organization in exchange for leniency from the government on their pot smuggling indictment. Unbeknownst to us at the time, their testimony before a grand jury brought an indictment against Morgan and me in 1981.

Deals were made by the government for the group's co-operation. Many went to prison with lengthy sentences, leniency to be given if and when Morgan and I were captured and found guilty. They would also be required to testify against us in court.

With new found knowledge about the island's operation, the U.S. was now pressing the Bahamian government with threats, insisting that they terminate the Norman's Cay operation. Through our connections, we learned that the plan was to place a permanent contingency of police in residence on the island. They were to be rotated frequently to deter corruption.

After much contemplation, Morgan made the decision to remove what assets were left on the island. With the boats and aircraft having already been disposed of, the Bahamian staff generously taken care of and returned to their respective native islands, Norman's Cay was closed down.

Sheldon and I thought about returning to our cozy cabin in Canada. Morgan requested that before we returned, we ac-company him one last time to Colombia for another visit, after which, he would see to it that we were delivered to any place of our choice.

The last few of us, with Norman in tow, loaded our most important possessions in one suitcase each aboard Sugar Charlie—Morgan's sleek long range Turbo Commander. We never looked back. The final chapter on Norman's Cay had been written, and the book was closed.

CHAPTER TWENTY

COLOMBIAN SOIL

ARRIVING IN COLOMBIA, we skipped the normal entry procedure, none of us immigrants having one shred of the required paperwork. We landed at the Armenia airport, this time without any fanfare. Not being an airport of entry, no customs paperwork was required.

Initially, we were guests of Morgan at "Bello Horizonte", his picture book ranch sitting on a bluff over-looking the verdant pastures in a valley below. Pure white cattle contently grazed in a pasture adjoining a large spectacular bamboo grove on one side, and hectares of pineapples on the other.

Jaime, a close friend of Morgan, who had been a guest on the island and now a very good friend of ours, invited us to be his guests at his chalet at an exclusive country club. We were welcome to stay as long as we desired. He was a cordial host, looking after our every need. I shall forever cherish the close friendships that I developed with my Colombian amigos.

We saw Morgan often when he had time to spare from his business activities. Being an ambitious and charismatic young man, he had a large following of admirers that encouraged him to enter the political arena in his local area. He was very adept at impromptu gatherings and speaking to his fellow countrymen. He was also busy completing a beautiful hotel that was built on the side of a mountain with a breathtaking view.

Morgan had purchased an old dairy farm and invited us to take a look at it. It was in close proximity to his hotel. It consisted of a farm house and a structure for feeding and milking the cows. The farmhouse was of typical design and construction used in the days when the milk and supplies were hauled by wagon to and from town. The bottom walls were built from bamboo posts with a mixture of cow manure, clay, and straw forming thick walls around the bamboo. The bottom floor served as a barn for livestock, plus two other rooms that housed the workers.

The second floor was constructed of lumber, and served as the owner's main living space. There was a wide porch that encircled the upper level. This overlooked the entire farm and provided a splendid view of the surrounding area. The old farm was a time honored structure with a striking personality; with a little imagination, it had great potential.

It was late September, around my birthday, and upon my congratulating Morgan on his latest acquisition, I was shocked when he told me that the farm was his birthday gift to me! I was more than shocked, I was overwhelmed! Sheldon and I need not concern ourselves with the other living options that we had been considering. Morgan had even taken care of our resident status and furnished us with a live-in helper.

Morgan was uneasy about us having a car and running around the country unescorted. For safety reasons, Morgan decided anything we needed would either be delivered, or we would be picked-up, and driven to whatever destination we desired. We were well taken care of indeed! At times I felt guilty about being a burden on our friends, but they seemed to take pleasure in helping us. Sheldon and I kept to ourselves in our new Colombian home, happily occupied, making a few changes for comfort.

CHAPTER TWENTY-ONE

GUERILLA TROUBLE

THERE WAS ONE particular group of guerrillas that assumed they could finance their covert activities by taking hostage rich drug dealers or their families and friends and holding them for ransom. Morgan was one of their first victims. He was captured at gunpoint by two of these rebels and forced into a waiting vehicle. He momentarily overwhelmed them and bolted out the door. He took a shot in the chest, knocking him off his feet, but he quickly got up and dashed into a nearby crowd of people, eluding his abductors.

Checking into a hospital, Morgan was informed by doctors that his wound was superficial. The bullet had hit him at an angle, glancing off a rib, and exiting a few inches from where it had entered.

This episode triggered a unification of the major drug dealers, dealing with the matter in short order, and effectively. During the conflict, families and friends were sent to other locations or put under heavy security. Our little farm was no exception. We were guarded twenty four hours a day. Morgan was concerned about our safety, our farm being easy to access. He requested that we temporarily relocate to a safer location, which turned out to be a large country home, walled like a fortress. It was located in a small village several miles from Bogota, a great distance from where the action was.

We were never to see our farm again, our circumstances having changed from a pleasant country lifestyle to having to hide from would-be abductors. It also became obvious that we were a burden to our dear friend Morgan, who had more important matters of concern than babysitting Sheldon, Norman and me.

On one of Morgan's visits to our stockade, we discussed the idea of leaving Colombia, and finding another island to live on. Morgan agreed that our situation had deteriorated considerably, and that under the circumstances, perhaps leaving would be better for everyone concerned. He suggested we relocate to Cartagena, where the finest marina in Colombia was located. It was there, he informed us, that the best opportunity to find a charter sailboat could be found. He put another friend in charge of driving us to Cartagena, and finding us an apartment near the marina. He stayed with us, tending to our every need, until we were familiar enough with the area and he felt we were comfortable taking care of ourselves. Before he returned to the "war zone", he left us telephone numbers where we could contact him at any time.

We became familiar faces at the marina, making an appearance almost every day. We were looking for any new arrivals that would be interested in chartering their boat to the South Pacific. Sheldon and I had selected this part of the world as our destination, our friend Jaime having made a trip there, and highly recommending it.

Months passed, and no prospects showed up. During this period in history, because of heavy drug trafficking, cruising boats usually gave Colombia wide-berth due to tales of pirates, boat confiscations, and harassment—all of which were most likely founded in truth, based on my own personal experience.

CHAPTER TWENTY-TWO

SOUTH PACIFIC BOUND

WHEN WE FIRST walked the marina docks at "Club de Pesca" to take a look at the local fleet, we noticed—anchored in the bay beyond the marina—an old wood hulled three-masted schooner. She was a hundred feet in length with masts as tall as she was long. Her name was "Serena", and you couldn't help but admire her beautiful lines and imagine the decades of high adventure she had experienced. She was a little shabby, in need of some TLC, but gorgeous and regal none-the-less.

At least once a day, weather permitting, her Skipper, a darkly tanned man, perhaps in his sixties, and his young first mate, would lower their dinghy over the side and row to the marina. His mate was an attractive lady who had the reputation of being a knowledgeable sailor herself. They would sip a cold beer while doing a little socializing at the local pub. They lived aboard the Serena and earned a little income taking tourists on an occasional day trip in the area.

One day, we struck up a conversation that led to the discussion of our plans. The Skipper mentioned that he would be interested in sailing us on his ship to the South Pacific and tour the area for as long as it took us to find what we were looking for. He had incurred a few debts locally since arriving a few months earlier. He didn't have the resources to pay them off, leaving them stuck in Colombia. He offered to take us wherever we wanted to go if we would pay off his debt and foot the expenses on the trip.

Sheldon and I were thinking more in terms of a modern forty footer for our journey; however, none had appeared on the horizon, and it was anyone's guess if and when one might show up. We discussed the possibility of the Serena and concluded that this was our only option. We struck a deal with the Skipper and said goodbye to our Colombian amigos. After paying off the local debt, we put on enough provisions to get us to Panama, and moved aboard.

The first mate recruited three crew members to sign on for the trip; the Serena being too large for only four people to safely and comfortably handle. Two of the crew were young Brazilian lads who spoke Portuguese and a smattering of English. The other young man was a Canadian from Alberta. He was homeward bound, having hitch-hiked from Canada to the tip of South America on the Pan American highway. All of his personal belongings were contained in his medium-sized backpack. None of them had ever been aboard any type of sailboat before.

The Skipper seemed anxious to weigh anchor as soon as possible. I was a little surprised when he announced, after putting all of our supplies aboard one morning, that we would be leaving that evening after dark. It was about nine that night when we quietly motored out of the harbor and set a course west—to the northern tip of Panama—about 350 miles away. This is where the city of Colon is located, and the entrance to the Panama Canal on the Caribbean side of Panama.

Being dark, and having an inexperienced crew aboard, we opted to motor instead of sailing all night. We took turns at the helm; with nothing more to do than maintain a compass heading. At sun-up, we were closing in on, and paralleling, the north coast of Panama—perhaps two miles offshore. We were approaching an archipelago of over 350 low lying cays. From a distance, they could only be distinguished by large groves of tall coconut palms rising above the horizon. The Skipper was familiar with this group of islands, referred to as "San Blas", and knew it to be inhabited by a colony of indigenous Indians called "Kunas".

This ancient tribe is known throughout the Caribbean for their beautiful and much sought after art work called "Molas". The Kuna women painstakingly produce these mainly for collectors. Their colorful and elaborate designs depict the flora and fauna that is found in and around their islands, and the dense jungle on the nearby mainland.

Folklore has it that in the not too distant past, the chiefs of this society decreed that to insure there was no cross breeding, no strangers were allowed on the islands after sunset. Anyone caught doing so would be stripped of all clothing and lashed with switches from a plant similar to poison ivy before being escorted off the island.

The Panamanian government permits the Kuna nation to self-govern to a certain extent. They also maintain an arts and crafts center in Panama City for the tribe to exhibit and sell their art work. The Kuna women's dresses are made from the same colorful artwork that is found in their molas, and are the subject of many tourists' cameras. Sheldon owned several examples of their most exquisite art work.

The Skipper suggested we pull in behind an island he had previously visited to spend a couple of days snorkeling on the shallow reefs in the warm crystal clear water. Being an avid diver, I jumped at the chance. It was then that we discovered the poor boating skills of our crew. We had to negotiate several narrow channels through the reef to reach an area large enough to accommodate a hundred foot vessel with about ten feet of draft. Twice, due to miscalculations, we grounded Serena on shallow reefs. It required a great deal of luck to finally reach our destination. A mask and snorkel dive under the boat revealed a few gouges in the thick wood keel, but nothing of any consequence.

The following day we had better luck as we departed our anchorage without any mishaps. The first mate took charge of raising our sails, which were made of antiquated material akin to heavy canvas. Lacking mechanical assistance, we never could have raised a hundred feet of sail up three separate masts without the effort of the three lads from Cartagena. We stopped at another island, the largest of the group, which was a port of entry into Panama. Checking into customs through this small outpost was an easy-going casual affair.

CHAPTER TWENTY-THREE

THE TROUBLE WITH SERENA

WE ARRIVED AT the harbor entrance to the Panama Canal in the late afternoon. With sails stowed, we motored to a remote area out of the way of the heavy traffic moving through the harbor. We secured the ship, dropped the dinghy alongside, and a few of us at a time rowed ashore to a landing that had showers available. With a limited amount of fresh water aboard the Serena, this discovery was a welcome luxury.

This side of the harbor had no shore facilities, so it was decided that we should move the Serena across the harbor and anchor her in front of the yacht club. Sheldon, the Canadian lad, and I stayed aboard, with the rest of the crew taking the dinghy to the yacht club for a night out with hot food and cold beer.

We noticed Serena's position was changing, and it appeared that we were dragging the anchor with the tide change. With the working crew ashore, we had to figure out how to weigh the anchor, start the engine, and relocate the ship.

It wasn't long after the rest of the crew returned that a harbor boat pulled up alongside and directed us to move our ship to a pier in the industrial area of the harbor. That's when we were boarded by Customs and Immigration officials. Having satisfied their cursory inspection, we were notified the Serena was being detained by a court order over a dispute about the ownership of the vessel. The alleged owner was on her way to Panama from Colombia. We were told that if she didn't show up within seventy-two hours, we were free to leave. It seemed that the Skipper had neglected to share this part of the story with us.

As it turned-out, the Serena was owned by a woman from the States. She had been a friend of the Skipper, as the story was told. The ship being idle and not earning her keep, the Skipper had proposed a business deal to her. He would sail her to the Caribbean, where the Charter business was supposedly lucrative, and after expenses were deducted, they would share the profits.

The information was vague as to what happened to the partnership. From all appearances, the Skipper dissolved it without her knowing and took off for parts unknown. When the owner finally figured out what had happened, she began a search, eventually discovering her boat was in Cartagena. I assume the Skipper found out she was hot on his trail, thus his necessity to hastily leave Cartagena before the posse showed-up. For some unknown reason, she didn't make the seventy-two hour deadline, and were we free to leave and transit the Panama Canal.

CHAPTER TWENTY-FOUR

STRANDED IN PANAMA

TAKING THE TRIP through the Panama Canal is quite an experience, certainly one that should be of high priority should the opportunity present itself.

After the proper paperwork is taken care of, you are assigned a transiting day and time. Upon arriving at the entrance to the lock, a canal pilot boards your vessel to assist you in the finer points of transiting—especially the locks procedure. The fifty mile trip across the isthmus usually takes eight to twelve hours. The pilot maintains residences on both sides of the canal, resting before returning on another vessel. All vessels are required to have line handlers aboard to secure the ship in the locks.

As our trip through the canal started, when we entered the first chamber, we somehow managed to run into the side of the lock. With much diplomacy, the pilot requested that any future maneuvering within the locks be handled exclusively by him.

The fifty mile trip across the Isthmus was interesting and beautiful. The shores of the lake were covered with dense jungle, possibly reminding one of what it might be like to navigate the

Amazon River. That daydream would immediately vanish when around the next bend; a "Love Boat" style cruise ship would suddenly appear with what seemed to be ten thousand tourists hanging from every nook and cranny. As we departed the first lock, we motored into the lake for an hour or so. Our pilot suggested that because we were making good time, that we tie up to a channel buoy out of the way of traffic, and take a refreshing dip in the cool waters of the lake. We all enjoyed this respite, including our beloved Norman. He had to be raised and lowered from the boat by a make-shift sling attached to a davit.

It was early evening and the sun was setting when we exited the last lock and headed for an island a mile or so offshore. There we would find an easily accessible anchorage to spend the night. A harbor pilot pulled up alongside the Serena, and our pilot, with his back pack in hand, jumped aboard, bidding us a fond farewell and a successful trip to the South Pacific. A very professional and personable chap indeed.

After running aground, or more accurately—through the mud, by accidently getting on the wrong side of well lit buoys-, we finally arrived at our destination where we dropped anchor, secured the ship, and turned-in. We placed our bunk mattresses on the deck; below decks being much too hot and humid to sleep, even as dead tired as we were.

It seemed that we had only been asleep for a few moments, when another boat pulled aside us and announced—with bull horns blaring—that they were the harbor police and were boarding our vessel. They told us that the owner of the Serena had arrived in town and obtained a court order for the police to seize the boat.

We had to gather up our belongings and were escorted to shore, where we were once again required to clear customs and immigration. Everything being in order, we were free to leave. The officer in charge arranged for a patrol car to drive us to a hotel in downtown Panama City.

The Skipper had an American friend, "Penny", who worked on a canal tugboat as an engineer. She lived in a predominately American area called Balboa. Penny seemed pleased to hear from the Skipper and offered to let us all stay at her place until we could get ourselves organized. The two Brazilian lads muttered something like "ship of fools" – and departed our company. The Canadian youngster stayed on to see if there was any chance we might end up finding a way to the South Pacific.

Within a couple of days, the Skipper had discovered that Serena's owner had flown in a crew from the states to sail her long lost ship back home. No charges were placed against him, but we were all stranded in Panama. He was apologetic for the way things turned-out, but I couldn't be angry, because Sheldon and I had already decided that to continue on would have been foolhardy, considering the condition of the Serena and the sorry experience of crew. We were ready to abandon ship anyway. We departed friends, never to see him again.

Sheldon and I needed time to sort out our sudden and unexpected change of plans. We didn't want to burden Penny any longer than it took to find a place we could rent by the month. She introduced us to a close friend named Bill, who was also a "Zonie", a name given to someone who lived and worked in the canal zone. This ten mile wide area encompassing the canal was controlled by the U.S. government. Bill took us under his wing and seemed to enjoy familiarizing us with the part of the world where he had been raised, his parents also being Zonies. He turned-out to be a helpful, kind and generous friend.

We found a place to live on the beach. It was no "Club Med", but it was out of the city, secluded and quiet; an acceptable place to temporarily lick our wounds and devise a new plan. The lad from Canada decided to return home. Once again, there were just the three of us continuing our adventure. We relocated two more times, each time improving our situation.

Sheldon and I considered our options. Returning to the war zone in Colombia didn't rate high on our list. The long trip back to our cabin in Canada didn't sound too bad, but we were happiest when we were near the ocean, and a no stress island life seemed most appealing. We contemplated checking the marinas in Panama to see if we could find a ride to the South Pacific.

Bill showed up one day to invite us for a weekend outing at a friend's beach house on an island on the Caribbean side of the country. We had forgotten that there was another ocean just fifty miles away, and we eagerly accepted his generous offer.

Bill picked us up; we purchased provisions for the weekend, and headed across the Isthmus. To my knowledge, there is no other road that crosses the country other than a mostly paved two-lane highway. A large part of the road was built in close proximity to the canal. Everywhere there was lush vegetation, with areas having been cleared to build small roadside communities. It was a beautiful exciting trip; the excitement being provided by drivers with nerves of steel, exhibiting their high-speed car passing techniques on a two lane road. NASCAR seemed tame by comparison.

A few miles before reaching Colon, on the Caribbean side, we turned off the "speedway" and took a road that would parallel the coast for some forty miles, terminating in a small village called Nombre de Dios. The two lane coastal road was poorly paved for about twenty-five miles; the pot-holed road turning into gravel at the beginning of the little village of Portobelo. We stopped in this quaint old native village for a cold beer, and to buy some ice for our coolers; this stop being the last place these were available.

We travelled beyond Portobelo for another ten miles or so, the road climbing over foothills and crossing rivers, all surrounded by dense rain forest which was part of a tropical jungle. We passed several more small coastal villages before arriving at our last stop—the village of La Guaira. Our destination—"Isla Grande"—was separated by a half mile wide channel from this village. To reach it, we had to negotiate with one of the local natives to ferry us across in an outboard driven cayuco, a primitive canoe.

Bill's friend's beach cottage was one of several houses located on one end of this mile long island. The other end was occupied by a small resort. It consisted of a half dozen beach cabanas, a restaurant, bar, quarters for the staff, and the owner's residence. Nothing fancy. No bells, no whistles, just a beautiful tropical setting, with someone to politely assist you if you requested it; otherwise, you were on your own. If you were to enter the small bar, you might be tempted to look around to see if maybe Humphrey Bogart was sitting in one of the comfortable bamboo chairs under a slow rotating ceiling fan.

The natives here lived in a small community in the middle of the island. The island generator was located there, as well as a few establishments where supplies could be purchased. There were no roads or vehicles; the length of the island spanned by one well used path. We were pleasantly impressed by this tiny beautiful island and its picture book resort. So much so, we made arrangements to rent the resort owner's house, which just happened to be available at the time.

We were smitten. A decision had to be made. If we were going to relocate to Isla Grande, we would need transportation. Buying a vehicle seemed foolish if our intentions were to head to the South Pacific; but after seeing the Caribbean side of Panama, we decided to stay where we were, sparing ourselves much expense, even though the trip could have been an unforgettable experience. We settled in our new found paradise and bought a small used station wagon.

Jack on Norman's Cay circa 1978 - 81

Remains of Carlos' Volcano House on
Norman's Cay 2009

Carlos Lehder (A.K.A.
Morgan) Credit: Sygma

Remains of C-46 in the Norman's Cay
lagoon. Iconic image of the island's colorful
history

Norman's Cay contraband

Jack, Sheldon and friends

Jack and his trusty
smuggling plane
Navajo N50RK on
Norman's Cay

Jack's smuggling plane in Colombia

Jack and Norman plotting a flight plan

Jack, Sheldon and Norman

Jack, the hippie
playboy

Jack celebrates the holidays

Jack at the helm in his
element

Jack in happier days

Jack sets world land speed records in the Silver Eagle 1971

Jack's prison years circa 1987 - 2009

Jack's prison ID - Federal Correctional Institution Memphis

Norman's Cay in the breathtaking Exuma chain in the Bahamas. Credit: Earthflight Media.

Aerials of Norman's Cay and its infamous runway. Credit: Earthflight
Media/Craig Peyton

SAMPLES OF JACK'S PRISON ARTWORKS

Smuggler's self-portrait. Jack and Navajo N5ORK

The C-46 over Norman's Cay

Carlos' famous Volcano House on Norman's Cay

Jack's favorite modern day plane PC-12

Gulfstream

Jack's secluded hut on the Caribbean coast of Panama

CHAPTER TWENTY-FIVE

BLUE LAGOON

WE WERE MORE than pleased with our decision to relocate to Panama's Caribbean side. Isla Grande was more like what we had in mind. The owners of the resort here were part of an influential Panamanian family, whose matriarch was the current mayor of Portobelo. Her free-spirited personable young son managed the resort. We hit it off well with this young man.

The local scuttlebutt had it that the resort was built by another man, an American, who had the dubious reputation of being a drug smuggler. After spending a great deal of time and money, he completed his project, using as much local labor as possible, making him popular among the natives.

Eventually, it is rumored that a powerful Panamanian politician informed the American that the government was looking into his suspected infamous career, and it appeared that he had a serious problem. As the story goes, he was told that if he was quick to leave the country, it was likely he could escape the forthcoming problems. The American heeded this advice, packed-up, and moved north one country to Costa Rica. Somehow, the high ranking official ended-up with the lad's resort.

During our stay at the resort, we became acquainted with not only most of the island residents, but with many in the community of La Guaira on the mainland. One person in particular, who was to become a close friend, came to our attention. He was a member of another influential family deeply involved in politics, himself having been a high-ranking official. He was well educated, multi-lingual, and had traveled the world. He had become involved in a scandal that a less important person would have gone to prison for. He was allowed his freedom if he would go into exile and maintain a low profile; thus, he ended up in the remote village if La Guaira. He had a modest home on several acres of beach front property, an old pick-up truck, and a local beer distributorship to provide him with income and a past time, other than chasing young native women and drinking a case of beer every day.

He had been there many years before we met him, becoming an authority on everything that went on in and around the area. Everyone knew him as "Poppi".

Apprising Poppi of our desire to find a home site, Sheldon and I were treated to his valuable guidance. He took us under his wing and let us erect a temporary shelter on his property while we searched the area for our own homestead. We soon discovered that in the wilderness areas, especially in third world countries, you cannot depend on real estate agencies for any type of assistance in locating and purchasing property. You must do it yourself. In our situation, it was either by boat or perhaps helicopter, the latter being out of the question.

After moving into our temporary location at Poppi's place, which consisted of a tent under a thatch roof, we hired a local native and his cayuco to help us scout the local area for a choice piece of property. Nothing excited us. We had to broaden our area of search. We decided that when we found what we were looking for, our means of transportation would be by boat. None of the coast was accessible by road, except for some of the small villages. To save time and money, we purchased our own boat and outboard motor. It was a twelve foot fiberglass skiff with a ten horse Mariner outboard.

For several weeks, we went on almost daily boating trips. We checked every small island, cove, nook and cranny. A few were okay, but not quite what we were looking for. We kept extending the length of our trips, until one day, we rounded the tip of a peninsula, and there it was—a secluded cove on the leeward side of the peninsula. The cove had a barrier reef extending across it, with a narrow channel through it that could be negotiated in a small boat if you paid close attention and went slowly. Between the inside of the reef and the white sandy beach was a blue lagoon, the water as clear as crystal.

The peninsula was the final extension of a mountain range that dropped abruptly into the sea. It had steep cliffs on the rough seaward side, with the lagoon on the sheltered leeward side. The peninsula was perhaps two hundred feet at its highest point, with an isthmus that graduated from sea level at the lagoon to about fifty feet high on the cliff side. The peninsula varied in width from a city block as its widest point to almost a hundred feet at the isthmus, and then tapered to a point where it ended. Except for the isthmus, the peninsula was covered in dense jungle with large trees. A few old coconut palms grew around the perimeter of the lagoon. There was a growth of mangrove that separated the lagoon from a much larger cove known as "Playa Blanca". This cove could accommodate half a dozen average sized sailboats.

CHAPTER TWENTY-SIX

PARADISE FOUND

POPPI ACCOMPANIED US to the area after we had made several trips to explore the property that had captured our hearts. We had decided that this was where we wanted to build our home. By speaking to a few of the natives that lived in the immediate area, the consensus was that the property belonged to an old woman who lived in Portobelo.

Poppi explained that in this part of the world, you dealt with whoever claimed possession of the property; the local natives not being literate in such matters as titles and deeds. To keep from causing any conflict with your neighbors, if more than one person claimed possession, it would be prudent to negotiate with all parties concerned. In this case, there was only the woman to deal with.

The natives here determine property value by how many coconut palms are on it. The coconuts are the only things on the land that have any value to them; and that is only when the large boats from Colombia show up twice a year and visit the coastal villages to purchase their crops. At that time, they were paying fifteen cents a nut.

A prime coconut palm was valued by the natives at ten dollars. This particular property had thirty-five palms in various stages of growth, only a few qualifying as prime trees. Giving the benefit of the doubt, the maximum value of the property should have been three hundred and fifty dollars.

Because her father had left her this property, the old woman claimed a sentimental attachment, even though she had never laid eyes on it. She waited several weeks for her husband to return from an extended timber cutting trip. Being anxious to acquire this property, I offered her ten times the going price, relying on her greed to overcome her sentimentality. My presumption was correct. The property would be ours, once we had a written agreement, which Poppi provided.

He recommended that on my next trip to town, I stop by a survey company and obtain an aerial photo of the peninsula. With the eight by ten in hand, we all met in Portobelo, and agreed where the property line would be. We inked a line across the photo, depicting the property line, with a signed agreement written on the back. A rough calculation by approximate measurements indicated that the property contained ten hectares—about twenty five acres. We and a witness from each party signed the agreement. The money was paid in crisp Benjamin Franklins, and the deal was done. As far as the native community was concerned, we were the new owners.

Thus, I embark on what would be the most rewarding and pleasurable chapter of my life, as I adopted a Spartan Robinson Crusoe type lifestyle. It is here, in a primitive Panamanian paradise, in an anti-establishment, remote, homesteading environment, that I finally find the high quality of life I had sought my entire life. While I may be considered an adventurous spirit, I think of myself as a hedonistic philosopher, always on the search for the pleasures of the mind and body—and it was here in Panama that I found them. For a reason unknown, I have been motivated all of my life to search for the answers to achieving this pleasure, which I refer to as 'quality of life'. This unrelenting search has led me through many trials and errors that most people tolerate and endure without any attempt to recognize the problems and correct them. Thus, my experience far exceeds that of the average person in this society.

This search for the truth/solutions to life's problems has prompted many of my peers to refer to me as a wise philosopher. In my journey, I have discovered many truths in my quest for happiness—all of them culminating with the solution to achieving the highest quality of life being directed to the "pampering of one's senses"—a phrase that I coined. For me, this entailed a radical departure from the mainstream to pursue its rewards.

Thus, I am a life explorer that makes every attempt to practice the truths that I have discovered, resulting in an inner peace that few of my peers neither understand nor enjoy. I am willing to share my discoveries with those that recognize the smile on my weathered face and the twinkle in my eye, but also content to let everyone pursue their own discoveries in their own time and manner.

As far as others are concerned, being a pleasure seeker, I have little endurance or patience with those that bring misery into my life and will seek a tactful way to disassociate myself from the source as quickly as possible.

Most people were my 'nemesis' when it came to quality of life. The pursuit of money was my Achilles heel, placing me in a position of having to deal with incompatible people in order to survive.

Ideally, money is a blessing to facilitate establishing a self-reliant lifestyle, so that you never have to depend on money again. That is the ultimate challenge and ambition.

Pleasure has a much higher priority than chasing or protecting the all mighty buck; part and parcel of the eccentric old pirate I am.

CHAPTER TWENTY-SEVEN

OUR HAPPY HUT

WE DECIDED TO build our small home on stilts in the lagoon, sitting on a shallow reef just offshore. Our home site was under a very old large tree that grew at the edge of the lagoon, with its root system snaking up the steep hillside behind it. The tree's canopy flared out and cascaded down to almost sea level, creating a giant umbrella effect; thus providing a shady and scenic home site. We would build our home without any disturbance to the tree. Our neighbors referred to this beautiful old tree as the "Iguana Tree". It did indeed provide a home and food for these large gentle reptiles. The tree provided seed pods once a year that attracted hundreds of small green parrots that chattered incessantly while stripping the pods of their tiny black seeds which were embedded in a fluffy material resembling cotton.

Our neighborhood consisted of native Panamanian and Indian families. Our Indian neighbors were of the "Choco" Tribe, originating in Colombia. They were illiterate and totally self-sufficient. They survived quite well by growing fruits, grains, and vegetables; with rice and coconuts being their staple foods. They were also excellent fishermen, and hunted when they could afford to buy a few bullets. One native family in particular was a great help to us. The father and the oldest son worked for us, usually one day a week, to earn a little income. They were to teach us many important things about nature survival skills and life in general.

We negotiated with a Panamanian from Isla Grande to build the basic structure of our home. He had built a few native homes but never one on stilts in the ocean. He and his crew would do the heavy work of cutting the posts and beams, and without any type of guide, cut the floor boards by a hand-held chainsaw. They used the same method for cutting the other necessary lumber to build a twenty foot square structure. When they were finished we had an elevated floor with personality—having a variety of thicknesses. At the highest tide, the floor was about five feet above water. The structure had a steeply pitched palm thatched roof covering it.

We moved our tent from our temporary camp at Poppi's to the floor of our new home. We finished the rest of the structure while living in it, and it turned out to be a project that was never quite finished. The longer we lived in it, the more comfortable and personable it became. It would become our beloved home.

Having to bathe and carry water from a small stream two blocks away inspired us, as our top priority, to dig a well in a low spot on the isthmus. It was hand dug—about six feet deep, eight feet in diameter and lined with loose stones. It gave us plenty of fresh water, even during the dry season. Water was retrieved by standing on a plank laid across the well and casting a five gallon plastic bucket, with a rope attached, into the water. Pulling it out when half full would keep the weight manageable. For as long as we lived there, this system never changed. Being in a hurry was never a consideration; our lifestyle being leisurely and consisting of only a few chores.

As time passed, we dug two more wells. One was cased in with cement blocks which we made. A couple of feet of sand was poured into the well, to act as a filter, the water having to enter through the bottom. This clean water was used for drinking and cooking. It was crystal clear, even during the rainy season, which made the other wells slightly muddy. The other well was dug in the garden for irrigation during the dry season. The original well was used for bathing, laundry, and doing the dishes. Norman got frequent rinses from this well. He might decide to take a dip in the lagoon several times a day. All of our bathing was done by retrieving the water as previously described and standing in an area covered with large gravel. With a bowl made from a large gourd, cool water was poured over us. Living in the tropics, hot water was never a consideration for any use, except cooking.

Having solved our water challenges, our next priority was to build a utility room on the isthmus. This was built of home-made concrete blocks, and was used as a tool shed and storage area that housed a small 3.5 kilowatt Lister generator. Not yet having discovered that we could very well do without electric gadgets, I felt it was necessary to have a generator. I went to a great deal of trouble and expense to acquire and have that generator delivered to our little homestead. To the dismay, I am sure, of our creature friends, I ran this noisy smelly machine every night for longer than I care to remember. This, so the paddle fan I had installed over our bed would make sleeping a bit more enjoyable. I finally came to my senses and made other arrangements.

Two other structures were ultimately built. One, on the beach, was rather primitive—made of driftwood, bamboo, and thatch. It was a guest hut, consisting of a bedroom and a toilet. It was quickly built for Sheldon's mom, who came to visit. She loved it so much, she wanted to stay. She was ill when she arrived, toting a bagful of medication. The leisurely no stress lifestyle rapidly cured her maladies; however, she grew depressed because she was lonely. We agreed to let her boyfriend from the states fly down to join her. After he arrived, all went well for a few months, but their relationship started to deteriorate, resulting in our having to ask them to leave.

The other structure we built was a small ten by twenty foot caretaker's cottage. It was also on stilts, elevating the cottage about two feet above the ground. It was located on the point of the peninsula, about a city block from our home. This was to be our garden and livestock area, known as "The Farm". It was built for a native friend named Trini who lived in a neighboring village up the coast about two miles. He was a likeable old man who spent most of his time fishing and telling stories. He and a friend would paddle their small cayuco over to our place at least once a week and share his folk lore with us. We would serve them a hot lunch which was always greatly appreciated. Sheldon's culinary delights were indeed a rare treat. Trini often discussed his expertise in raising livestock, especially pigs and chickens. We decided it might be to our advantage to have him living on the property, raising a few pigs and chickens, selling enough to cover his expenses. Trini could also maintain our small banana and coconut groves; thus, a deal was struck. The caretaker's house was built, and he moved on.

We purchased the livestock, and turned the program over to Trini. Only a couple of months passed before it became obvious that Trini's forte was story-telling, and that he knew less about raising livestock than Sheldon and I did. Except for a few chickens, and one pig, we liquidated the rest of the livestock and let him remain to assist in maintaining the property.

CHAPTER TWENTY-EIGHT

SIDESTEPPING SOCIETY

WE HAD LIVED here long enough to become familiar with our area and most of the creatures we shared it with. The time arrived when I developed a sense of appreciation and respect for my creature friends, and became very protective of them. I established a rule that our neighbors were welcome on our property, but hunting was prohibited. Our property had become a refuge for whatever wanted to visit or live here.

Trini was the first person to challenge this new rule. For some reason, perhaps his native instincts, he could not resist the temptation to kill an animal for food if the opportunity presented itself. After a few incidents, and my expressing my extreme displeasure with his conduct, he pushed me beyond my limit of tolerance by slaying a young pregnant deer. His career of being our caretaker was terminated, and we requested he vacate the premises.

Our property was home to white tail deer; pacas, a very large rodent; sloths, a slow moving tree dweller; coatis, a South American raccoon; Howler Monkeys; iguanas; possums; and ocelots, although we never had the pleasure of seeing these small shy cats. There were lots of birds, most unknown to us, but we did recognize the Pelicans that fished the lagoon, and the families of Toucans and Parrots.

Boa Constrictors lived in our dense jungle, as well as the Fer-de-Lance, the only poisonous snake known to live in this area. We did observe many harmless snakes of various sizes and colors, including a rather large beauty that occasionally visited our home to dine on the mice that had built their nests in our thick thatch roof.

As one might suspect, there was a huge insect population with mosquitoes prevailing. Ones to be wary of were hornets, scorpions and spiders. There was a dangerous brilliantly colored caterpillar that I had the misfortune of accidently touching one day. The immediate and extreme pain was almost unbearable until I could scrub the area with wet beach sand. It was more painful, if that is possible, than a stingray puncture I had once experienced.

Our barrier reef surrounding the lagoon supported a huge population of resident tropical fish, the likes of which would make an aquarium aficionado green with envy. Some notable inhabitants were lobster, octopus, and eels, with transient visits from sharks, rays, barracudas, and turtles. A school of snappers lived on the reef beneath our house. We threw them snacks from our porch which they devoured with great gusto. We became such good friends that they would often accompany me on my daily snorkeling trips out to the reef.

Edible plants native to this area were coconuts; yuca, a starchy root used like potatoes; platinos, a large cooking banana; citrus fruit; avocados; mangoes; large papayas; pineapples; and bread-fruit. Many other plants also thrived including coffee and cacao.

Our home was built with half walls enclosing the living area, with a three-foot wide porch encircling the entire structure. A ten by ten foot porch was later added to the front of the house for lounging and accommodating Sheldon's container plants. The porch was open on all sides and had a clear plastic roof. There were no windows or shutters in our home, allowing any breeze to freely circulate. Rainfall, accompanied by strong winds, was subdued by unrolling split bamboo curtains suspended from the eaves of the roof.

Our living area consisted of one corner dedicated to our kitchen. A U-shaped counter bordered three sides of this area. One section of counter was tiled and used for cooking, a two burner hotplate doing a splendid job of it. It was fueled with propane as was our small refrigerator which eventually saw little use due to our eating most of what we cooked; thus not having to preserve leftovers. The cost of operation didn't justify keeping cold drinks and making ice cubes.

The other two counters were used for meal preparation and eating, with one having an attached bench. An oven, from an apartment sized stove, was located under the hotplate counter. This was used for baking; usually cornbread, made from fresh ground cornmeal, baked in a cast iron skillet.

Shelves under one counter held all of our utensils, except those few that hung from a ceiling joist.

Next to the kitchen area was the only floor to ceiling wall, which supported open shelves used for storing sealable containers to protect our food supply. High humidity and sea salt in the air took its toll on everything except plastic.

Our bed, a foam rubber mattress, occupied another corner, and was elevated about four feet off the floor. It had shelves beneath that accommodated clothing and linens. The bed, elevated to wall height, allowed unobstructed access to any breeze that might pass through.

The remaining corner was left open; the main entry into the living area located here. A hammock hung on a corner post. It could be stretched across the area and hooked up in a moment. I couldn't begin to calculate the number of hours I spent there, contemplating my exemplary lifestyle.

The porch around the house had railings or shelves, one section of shelves used for a dishwashing area. Other shelves contained potted plants and a large birdhouse. This was constructed for a toucan fledgling that Sheldon acquired from a native. It lived there until it was able to fend for itself, and then was free to do as it pleased during the day, returning in the evening to sleep.

We had an outhouse type of toilet at the rear of the house. It was constructed of bamboo and had a thatched roof. The door and walls were tall enough to allow privacy, yet not obstruct the view. The only other door in the house was a gate that separated it from the fifty-foot long bridge attached to the shore. This gate was more for looks than security; the chickens, possums, and anything else that wanted in being easily able to do so. The bridge was built detached from the house, thus deterring crawling insects like ants and scorpions from entering.

Above the corner of the house where the hammock was located, we built a small loft. It was large enough to hold a small foam rubber mattress in the event a visitor showed up. It had a large wood shutter that could be opened for light and a breeze. Storage was the loft's main purpose.

Most of the house remained the same over the years that we lived in it; the layout being simple and efficient. Changes or additions were to enhance its personality using cane and bamboo. Occasionally, during the night, the tide flowing into the lagoon would carry a stray log and we would be awakened by the log thumping against one of our house stilts. I would use a long slender length of bamboo, which hung from the eaves, to push the log away from the house. The next day, I would beach the log, until I had several to dispose of. On a calm day, I would roll all of the logs into the water and individually swim them through the channel in the reef, out past the point of the peninsula, into the current. This would carry them to other destinations.

The original roof was thatch, made from palm fronds. Cockroach droppings became difficult to deal with and the decision was made to replace the thatch with corrugated zinc roof. It wasn't as aesthetically pleasing, but considerably more practical. I often thought the zinc, covered with the thatch, might suffice.

CHAPTER TWENTY-NINE

HOMESTEADING

I T TOOK US a couple of years to get really comfortable in our home and get acquainted with the area. Being a homesteader requires a completely different mindset than living in the establishment. To achieve the maximum benefits, it requires a dedication to simplicity and self—sufficiency. Even if you had an unlimited source of income to purchase "necessary" things, you would still have to leave your cozy nest and deal with the establishment at some point—that being the source of necessary things. This is the main cause of your problems, and the reason for homesteading to begin with. A trip into town for me to purchase something that I deemed absolutely necessary was a tedious, depressing way to spend a day.

The side of Panama that I lived on is rather primitive. Supplies are limited and basic. So when I needed to buy essentials—like a part for my generator, I must make a trip to the "big city"-about a hundred miles away. If I don't want the grief and expense of spending the night away from home, I must be extremely well organized to pull it off in one day. A little luck helps, too!

An early departure is necessary, having prepared my outboard skiff for the trip the day before. I have to take along my establishment clothes to change into after my wet boat trip to the village, where I will leave my boat and catch a local bus or truck traveling the coast road. Bare feet, with threadbare cutoffs and a straw hat, is not acceptable attire from this point on. If I'm lucky, some means of transportation will pick me up within a few minutes. It will stop and pick up passengers, like myself, for the twenty-five mile trip to the main highway that crosses the isthmus. At this point, I get off, my coast transportation heading in the opposite direction.

Experience has taught me to pass up all opportunities for a ride until an "express" bus shows up. This intersection is the only stop this bus makes, until approximately one hour later when it arrives on the other side of the country—my destination. You can imagine the skill required to negotiate a "Greyhound" style bus for fifty miles on a two lane highway in about an hour. It seems to me these skillful drivers missed their calling.

Departing the bus in the city, I hail a small cab. Without stopping for lunch, I make a dash for the store that has the part I need. It might close-up shop for a two-hour lunch, as many small businesses are prone to do in Third World Latin American countries. Having my new part in hand, I now reverse the procedure to return home. Not knowing how long I will have to wait for an express bus heading back, or a coastal bus to my village, I dare not take the time to do any other shopping.

What a splendid feeling it is to round the last corner of the bay in my little skiff, and see the peninsula in the distance where my home and loved ones are waiting, while silently hoping that I won't have to repeat this journey any time soon. I could have spent the day with Sheldon and Norman, perhaps a leisurely stroll through our coconut and banana groves; more than likely, a little snorkeling in my giant maintenance fee aquarium before taking a little siesta in my hammock, gently swaying in the afternoon breeze. I wonder, is it really necessary to have electricity?

"Oh, once in your life you find someone
Who will turn your world around
Bring you up when you're feelin' down
Yeah, nothin' could change what you mean to me
Oh, there's lots that I could say
But just hold me now

"Baby you're all that I want
When you're lyin' here in my arms
I'm findin' it hard to believe
We're in heaven
And love is all that I need
And I found it there in your heart
It isn't too hard to see
We're in heaven"

-Bryan Adams, HEAVEN

"I proudly confess to being a hedonist, but feel that my delight in pleasure applies to all parts of life—not primarily to the gratification of lust—which appears to be the conventional interpretation of the word; however, I may be found first in line at the doorway to sensuous pleasure."
-JCR

CHAPTER THIRTY

PAMPERING THE SENSES

HAVING HAD THE outstanding experience of living in the rainforest of Panama for many years, I have come to the conclusion that my top priority for the highest quality of life is to keep everything simple in a safe, comfortable home environment where I can grow my own food. In fact, I had become so successful at this, I managed to reduce my reliance on money to about five hundred dollars a year. I am very low maintenance, requiring only the basic needs of life to be happy. I don't collect junk, try not to waste more than is necessary, and make every attempt to be a responsible steward of the earth.

By sharing this lifestyle with Sheldon, I discovered that I don't require more than one person to give my love and devotion to. Any neighbors that shared my lifestyle ideas would be an asset, but not a necessity. There would be much leisure time for play, after the few chores were taken care of. By play, I mean enjoying the treasures that nature provides; these far exceeding the "bells and whistles" that I relied on for pleasure while living in the establishment for forty-five years.

My former tenure as a weekend race car driver (smuggling pot out of Mexico as a renegade pilot was my weekday job), which afforded me the opportunity to set world land speed records in the electric powered Silver Eagle dragster in 1971, while exciting at the time, paled in comparison to the fulfillment I have found in my Robinson Crusoe type lifestyle. Looking back, I must confess that racing was more about ego gratification than anything else. I enjoyed the attention it brought me—attracting the ladies in droves; but that reward (which fed my incessant hunger for lust) really didn't make up for all the long hours and hard work my racing demanded. In fact, it was the Eagle project that motivated me to give up all competition. I had gone faster than anyone else in history in an electric powered car and my ego was satisfied. I knew I was the best. When I drove those top fuel dragsters and winning my fair share, the only pleasure I gleaned was the macho race car driver attention—mostly from the female race groupies. The rest of the racing game was tedious hard work. My ego had its fill.

In our homesteading paradise, I never longed for those days, or any others I had spent in the establishment. Not once did I miss the days of lounging on the couch, watching Saturday Night Live, and devouring junk food—which was the norm my former wives and I had regularly engaged in for entertainment. All that went away. So did my vanity. As a ladies' man, there was a time when I preened myself like a proud peacock—for the same lustful reasons that I assume everyone does. When I side-stepped society to live like Robinson Crusoe, being fit came naturally and being handsome was no longer important.

Examining the question of raising children, based on previous experience, I conclude that "establishment" children are a liability, not an asset. I believe that those that disagree with my assessment haven't taken the time to evaluate their true relationship with their children. It's really quite simple when you ask yourself the question of how much pleasure they provide you compared to the grief, which includes much worry and great expense – continuing until your demise. In your golden years, when your energy wanes, your lovely darlings will have the same responsibilities that you did at their age, and will be much too busy to provide you with the TLC that dignifies your station in life.

On the other hand, in an anti-establishment lifestyle, I see the possibility of a child being a potential asset by becoming a constant and loving companion. You would teach him your philosophy and values to be independent and free. He would become your apprentice, and assist you in maintaining mutual lifestyles. When your golden years arrive, your life's work and achievements will pass on to your adult child who loves it as much as you do. Your descendant will hold you in high esteem, and take delicate care of you until you view your last sunset from your front porch. I see this as being a win-win proposition, both you and your offspring having become assets to each other. From what I understand, many Amish and Mennonites use this theory quite successfully. A far cry from the conventional option.

Whether you are a billionaire in the establishment or a successful self-sufficient homesteader, good health is an absolute necessity for the highest quality of life. Plain and simple, without good health, life will never attain its potential. Anyone with just a smattering of common sense has to know that continually exposing one's body to contaminated food, water and air, and excessive stress, is not conducive to maintaining optimum health.

Reviewing our homesteading lifestyle, I can enthusiastically say that I had never been healthier or happier. Our food was nutritious and exceptionally delicious. Our water was clean and sweet, not even a hint of chorine or fluoride. The stench of exhaust smoke was non-existent in our air. The sounds of nature are what we became accustomed to. A siren was never heard, and the rare sound of a motor was for only a few moments as a boat passed by. Stress was non-existent, there being no one around except Sheldon, Norman, and an occasional welcome neighbor or visitor. News from the establishment never found its way to us; therefore, we were spared the negativity that so often taints society.

In sustaining the highest quality of life, a lasting love connection is a necessity. My love relationships while living in the establishment were without exception—a failure. After the honeymoon was over, and the passion subsided, we were basically just two strangers that shared a house and had little in common. Sleep and working at different jobs left little time to develop a friendship. The stress of society takes its toll! Some people just tolerate these circumstances. Most call it quits and move on, only to repeat the scenario, as I did.

And then there's the issue of lust. In the establishment, it was, without question, my nemesis.

The inborn lust (sexual desire) of all human beings—this persistent urge—is best enjoyed when the arousal is so exciting, that it's almost heart-stopping. Generally, this exhilaration is the primary motivation in new relationships and often results in living together or marriage, under the misunderstood pretense of love. It is only a question of time before FAMILIARITY erodes the original stimulation, but the desire for the sexual excitement remains. This is where the problem begins, when the craving for this excitement becomes overwhelming. In most relationships, every erotic idea that is MORALLY ACCEPTABLE has been attempted, and with no solution available, the grass starts to look greener on the other side of the fence and the eyes start to stray, looking to new sexual conquests. This is not limited to macho males, but enthusiastically pursued by the ladies, lust knowing no boundaries for masculine or feminine genders.

Once I became an ex-pat and chose an anti-establishment lifestyle, I discovered the secret to this dilemma—and that is for both parties in a relationship to come to an understanding that they are more than friends or lovers, they are a TEAM. They are a team in their quest for a higher quality of life—living outside of the establishment and pampering their senses, which includes their sexual gratification.

Exercising this theory, Sheldon and I became each other's best friend. We shared the same goals and challenges; we faced them and overcame them together as we worked side by side for our mutual well-being.

Love is the primary goal. A cozy home—the ultimate destination and sanctuary—is necessary for the soul's contentment. The natural instinct of lust must be satisfied to perpetuate the emotion of love. In the establishment, sexual desire is often relegated to the depths of vulgarity by a misguided culture. For most people, personal fantasies are just too shameful to share with a lover—but this was not the case for Sheldon and me. We shared all of our sexual fantasies with each other, regardless of the scandalous shame associated with it by society. We were open, honest and vulgar about what turns each of us on.

Once we shared our inner secrets and desires with one another, the cultural stigma of sexual conduct disappeared, and the excitement really begins. We became each other's co-conspirator, an ally; as both of us conspired together on how to realize our wildest and most risqué sexual fantasies together. This creates a unique and stable bond. Only your imagination will limit the exhilarating entertainment that can be experienced together.

Guilt, shame, jealously and deceit—that commonly sour traditional relationships—disappear. Sheldon and I ended up with a bond that was enduring, with a deep love unmatched in society. Who could ever replace a true friend like this rare treasure?

Establishment lifestyle relies on outside sources for almost all of its requirements for survival, necessitating the production income. This becomes the challenge of those involved in the relationship—requiring their separation, spending only a few hours together each day, with little quality time. This, combined with the stress of earning income, will eventually erode the relationship.

A common goal off "pampering one's senses" will eventually lead to abandoning the establishment lifestyle, where it's not possible to obtain such luxury; in favor of the alternative—a simple, self-reliant lifestyle in close proximity to the grandeur of nature.

Therefore, I have discovered the key to a successful relationship is dependent on a calculated plan of action including three absolute prerequisites: an anti-establishment lifestyle; autonomy in the relationship; and the knowledge to satisfy the cravings of lust. This means the freedom to pursue erotic pleasures together—with the common goal of quality happiness—creating a bond that few relationships can equal as trusting and loving best friends that happily cater to each other's titillating desires. This includes the naughtiest sexual pursuits to satisfy the demands of lust whenever our mutual mood strikes us. These lascivious occasions are planned and executed by Sheldon and me for maximum pleasure achieved. A very exciting undertaking that bolsters our love and devotion for each other! Thus, I discovered a lasting lust by satisfying it through living out our lewd fantasies together, rather than letting it perish through boredom and familiarity. On occasion, this involved erotic threesomes; intimately sharing Sheldon with my best friend Morgan in trysts we all eagerly participated in. Such sexcapades accommodated voyeurism with mutual consent. All of these ingredients concocted the potent cocktail that allowed Sheldon and me to achieve an exciting and enduring relationship. Once you experience a relationship like this, all others seem dull and insignificant by comparison.

So, yes, I proudly confess to being a hedonist, but feel my delight in pleasure applies to all parts of life—not primarily to the gratification of lust—which appears to be the conventional interpretation of the word; however, I may be found first in line at the doorway to sensuous pleasures.

I am certain that there must be others that have the same hedonistic desires that I am servant to, but in my comprehensive experience, I have not had the pleasure of meeting these creative souls. This is likely the result of being rather reclusive and not extensively known.

CHAPTER THIRTY-ONE

CHAOS CRASHING

FROM TIME TO time, we had company in our remote little piece of paradise. Beside Sheldon's mom and her boyfriend, other visitors to our home included Dyan, who, it seems, had participated in almost every phase of our adventure.

There was one other visitor who played a very important role in this story. I have saved him for last. He went by the name of "Jim". Jim was an acquaintance of Sheldon's mom when she lived in Arizona. He was a "two bit" drug dealer that supported Mom's habit. I am fairly confident she was not aware that Jim was also an undercover agent for the government.

Mom had albums of photos of her visits on Norman's Cay that were seen by Jim during one of his drug deliveries. The photos didn't show anything incriminating, but Morgan and I were included in her collection. There's a strong possibility that Mom embellished the story of Norman's Cay. She mentioned that she would soon be visiting us in Panama.

Slick Jim talked Mom into letting him accompany her to Panama, with the provision that he would not come to our home without our permission. When Mom showed up alone, she explained the circumstances, and we agreed to let him come to our home.

It should be clarified at this point, that I had no idea that I had been indicted in 1981 with Morgan. You may be assured that had I been aware of this information, NO Americans would have known where I lived.

Jim was treated cordially during his brief stay. Upon returning to the States, he promptly reported our location to the FBI; and because it was obvious that we weren't involved in any illegal activities in Panama, no action was taken to apprehend me at that time. It was later revealed that the DEA let me sit until Morgan was apprehended, which was a year and a half after Jim had informed them of my location. The government assumed that because Morgan and I were close friends, I was privy to much information, and therefore was destined to be a prime witness against him. They speculated that I would cooperate with them to save myself.

With Mom's history of erratic behavior toward me and track record as my adversary through-out the progression of my relationship with her daughter; you may wonder why I would allow her in my home. Even though Sheldon had long claimed to "hate" her "bitch" mother, she missed her, and had encouraged such visits. Not wanting to disappoint the best friend I dearly loved, I succumbed to her wishes. While I may never know if Mom's jealously over my relationship with Sheldon contributed to her bringing a DEA agent to my home, I do know that it was my desire to please Sheldon that allowed this fiasco to unfold. I do not blame my darling Sheldon for any of this, and take full responsibility for my actions. I was reckless in allowing her mercurial mother to enter my private paradise. This foolishness had deep roots in lust (remember—my initial interest in Sheldon, eleven years earlier, was largely influenced by my lustful attraction to an affectionate young virgin); and then there was her mother's ensuing jealously and wrath. Therefore, I must admit, lust played a contributing role in my downfall, eventually leading authorities to my whereabouts in Central America.

CHAPTER THIRTY-TWO

KIDNAPPED

THUS, THE FATEFUL day of February 4th, 1987 arrived. To say that I was in shock when the DEA kidnapped Sheldon and me is an understatement. I can think of no word that adequately describes how I felt for an extremely long time.

After being illegally apprehended in Panama, Sheldon and I are forced into an aircraft bound for the U.S. The story continues with our plane arriving and taxiing to a secure area at the Jacksonville, Florida airport. There were a half dozen people waiting for our flight to arrive. DEA agents quickly handcuffed and shackled me, placed me in a vehicle, and drove to a small country town about thirty miles west of Jacksonville. I was taken to a county jail reminiscent of "Mayberry USA", where I was deposited in a holding cell by myself. Being in shock, and completely exhausted, I feel asleep almost immediately.

I was to find out much later that Sheldon had been taken to a motel where she reported that she had been treated well until she could contact her family for assistance. I was pleased to discover this, but puzzled that she managed to escape any questioning or harassment. I never did find out the reason for this fortunate turn of events.

CHAPTER THIRTY-THREE

IN CUSTODY

THE PART OF the story I am about to relate is factual, as is all of the proceeding—and is considerably different than what was portrayed by the government to the media. This was a very high profile trial, my friend Morgan being the first Colombian cartel member to be apprehended and extradited to the U.S. to stand trial. Medellin Cartel was a name selected by the U.S. government to give the impression that there was an agreement between a group of Colombian drug dealers organized to control prices, production, and distribution of cocaine coming from Colombia; thus creating a monopoly and providing the government with reason to declare that the Cartel was responsible for eighty percent of the cocaine entering the United States. At no time was I aware of any such agreement; every producer being an independent entrepreneur, controlling their own markets and prices. The source of most of this information, which was misleading, was conjured up and furnished to the media by the shrewd prosecutor of our trial. It was later determined that he had ambitions of running for the U.S. Senate in Florida—hopefully, with a successful prosecution of a Medellin Cartel kingpin to bolster his campaign.

He skillfully orchestrated this trial to be the longest, most publicized drug trial in the history of this country. The trial had duration of over eight months, with well over a hundred witnesses taking the stand for the government. It cost the taxpayers several million dollars. Then there were the fines and income taxes owed on drug profits that were forgiven for many of the co-conspirators that agreed to snitch and testify for the government. This is not to mention the several thousand years of pardoned prison time for the same individuals. Lest you think that this is an exaggeration, all of this information is a matter of record if you know where to look.

CHAPTER THIRTY-FOUR

COERCION AND CONSTITUTIONAL LAW

IN THE FEDERAL Judicial System, an indictment is a document prepared by the prosecutor stating what the government alleges the defendant is guilty of. It is then submitted to a grand jury, which consists of twenty-three people who are supposed to be randomly selected to hear a one-sided argument by the government. The defendant is not given an opportunity to present a defense to the government's accusations.

The Federal government boasts of a 98% conviction rate, meaning that 98% of the people they arrest end up in prison, or under some type of supervision; the latter being dependent on how much assistance they have been to the government.

Coercion—more commonly known as "blackmail",which is a felony for anyone but the government—is standard procedure for the system. It accounts for the extremely high rate of convictions.

In my particular case, if I plead guilty to the charge against me, the prosecutor would make arrangements through a technical procedure with the court to show leniency in my potential sentence. If I agree to tell everything I know about Morgan and my co-conspirators, I receive even kinder treatment. Maximum benefits, depending on my value, would be given for all of the above, plus testifying for the government at trial. Conversely, if I exercised my right to be tried by a jury of my peers, and I am found guilty, I could be assured that I would receive the maximum penalty, along with the wrath of the court. I was informed of these options by both the prosecutor and the DEA.

For a defendant who has close ties with family, the scenario frequently gets worse. One of my co-defendants was facing a twenty-year sentence for her part in the conspiracy. As an added inducement for her cooperation, she was threatened with having her four year-old son taken away from her and placed in a foster home. She was put in a position of having to choose between me—a friend—and her son. After her testimony against me, she was released on probation.

Another often used ploy is to threaten to bring parents or other close family members into the conspiracy; this, for accepting or enjoying the pleasures of your ill-gotten gains. The government has plenty of offenders waiting in various institutions to do whatever is necessary to gain relief. The transcripts from my trial bear out all of the above; our defense attorneys having gleaned this information from the government's witnesses on cross examination.

With this kind of coercion prevalent in the existing system, it becomes obvious how the government can claim its 98% conviction rate, with only a handful of people exercising their right to a trial, all others pleading guilty and making a deal.

Few offenders are apprehended committing a crime. They are usually told on by co-conspirators who assist the government in setting a trap to catch them. This is called "Entrapment" which was against the law. An additional law, "Reverse Sting", was created to overcome this problem, thus making entrapment legal. Another major discrepancy in the system, and one of the worst, is the strict prohibition by the court of letting the jury know the power and responsibility it has by law. Any attempt to inform them will bring the fury of the court in the form of contempt or jury tampering. Even though most people believe that they have Constitutional rights, in a Federal Court, cases are determined by complicated one-sided statutes that favor the government. An attorney is an "Officer of the Court". Anyone who attempts to present a defense using the laws set forth in the Constitution will find themselves in disfavor, not only with the court, but with the American Bar Association. I was given this information when I requested my attorney to prepare my defense using Constitutional law. He flatly refused, saying he would be "blackballed" and may possibly lose his license. These represent only a few of the obstacles a defendant is faced with.

CHAPTER THIRTY-FIVE

CHARGED

I WAS CHARGED WITH conspiracy.

It is used as a catch-all and is most difficult to overcome. A conspiracy consists of two or more people making plans to break a law, whether or not they actually perform the act. Anyone who points a finger at you is sufficient to get you indicted. Think again if you believe you are "innocent until proven guilty". In reality, once you're accused and arrested, only a small percentage are allowed to make bond, so that you can remain free to conduct your life and prepare your defense, until your day in court arrives. The prosecutor's typical argument in a bond hearing is that you are a menace to society and a flight risk. This argument usually prevails, unless you decide to be a very helpful friend of the government. If you are able to prove in an evidentiary hearing that you are indigent (as I did), and can't afford an attorney, the court will appoint one for you. It is my understanding that they are selected from some type of pool. In my second trial, the first attorney who was appointed to represent me said the court must have made a mistake.

"Certainly they don't expect a real estate attorney to preside in a high profile criminal case." He was dismissed and a criminal attorney was assigned. These types of illogical events are not uncommon in the system.

CHAPTER THIRTY-SIX

MEDIA CIRCUS

THE SEQUENCE OF events that constitute a Federal trial starts off when authorities have reason to suspect you have broken a law. Except for small time street drug dealers, seldom do the police actually catch someone in the act of committing a crime. Usually someone who knows of your crime informs the police of your complicity. There are exceptions, but they are few. Informants are usually offenders in trouble looking for a way out; many times embellishing the facts of the crime. Another culprit might be a person who you have had a falling out with and wants some type of revenge. And of course, there are the law-abiding citizens that feel it is their duty to report any suspicious activity.

Once you are a suspect, a U.S. Attorney, who is also the prosecutor for the district where the alleged crime took place, takes the information before the grand jury to determine if there is enough evidence against you to bring an indictment. When an indictment is returned, it allows the police to arrest you and hold you for trial. Grand juries in this age generally haven't a clue about their true function, and invariably "rubber stamp" whatever is brought before them by the prosecutor. Grand juries are a formality; an excellent concept in its original form, but today, only a vague remnant of days long past.

In my first trial, I was accused and indicted by the grand jury for the conspiracy of importation (smuggling) of an illegal substance (cocaine) into the United States. The maximum penalty, if found guilty, was fifteen years in prison, and a twenty-five thousand dollar fine. The sentencing laws in effect at that time included the possibility of parole, which I would have been eligible for after serving one-third of my sentence (five years). Barring that possibility, if I was an exemplary prisoner, I would be credited with "good time" and released after serving two-thirds of my sentence (ten years).

My charge in the indictment amounted to one short paragraph, alleging that, "As an agent for Carlos Lehder Rivas (Morgan), I told the Jacksonville, Florida smuggling group to leave Norman's Cay; this, to further Morgan's cocaine smuggling operation".

Morgan, being the "Kingpin" in the indictment, received much more attention than I. He was accused of a Continuing Criminal Enterprise, which carries a maximum life sentence. He was also charged with nine separate conspiracies, each of which carries fifteen years. He had the potential combined sentence of life plus one hundred and thirty-five years.

The prosecutors could have written screenplays for fantasy movies. Beside daily press releases, stories were leaked out, without any credence, regarding Morgan's supposed notoriety and potential threat. There were unfounded rumors about a thirty-five hundred man army that was being smuggled into the U.S. to rescue him. There was the possibility of Colombian guerillas destroying a sports arena in Jacksonville during a major game, and other preposterous rumors.

The government became so fearful of this peaceful, charismatic young man—a person whose fellow countrymen loved and politically supported—that they felt it necessary to place Morgan in a maximum security prison. They transported him in military helicopters to and from court for pretrial hearings. There was no parking allowed on any of the main streets of Jacksonville within a city block of the courthouse when Morgan was in town. And to make sure the courthouse was secure—everyone entering was screened; this, long before any terrorist threats. A heavily armed SWAT team was stationed on the roof of the courthouse. A major prejudice against both of us was soon established in Jacksonville and the surrounding area, the very same area where the trial jury would be selected.

Morgan was commonly characterized by the media as a murderous villain and political screwball who boasted that cocaine was a 'Latin American time bomb'. Stories defined Carlos Lehder as a raging cocaine-crazed drug czar who would do anything to protect his business operation on Norman's Cay. The Carlos—or "Morgan", I knew, was a peaceful man.

Personally, I scoff at the frequently portrayed violent drug lord that he is purported to be—and his supposed involvement with Pablo Escobar's extreme violence is out of the question—unless Carlos managed to deceive me for the many years of our close friendship. That's a possibility but not a probability.

Because my role in the organization was—by choice—as a pilot only, and I resided on the island, my relationship with Pablo and other customers was very limited. Carlos did the negotiating while I snorkeled on the reef in front of my little hacienda. My business (smuggling) trips to Colombia were more like a NASCAR pit stop than my leisure visits, which were with Carlos' family and closest friends, and were not involved in the business. In Colombia, it was common knowledge that Pablo loved his country and his paisanos, but despised the corruption of his government. He was an intelligent and ruthless adversary of not only the government, but many of the contrabandistas. Pablo was considered a hero of many in Medellin—especially the poor. He was known as a rich narcoterrorist who boasted a Robin Hood image from his propensity to distribute money to the poor through housing projects and civic activities that made him so popular with the downtrodden. But Pablo's violent acts towards his foes stained that Robin Hood image, thanks to all the bloodshed he orchestrated, branding him a brutal and merciless killer.

I asked Carlos about how he managed to deal with Pablo's violent nature. After we moved to Colombia from Norman's Cay, the two of them had had a confrontation regarding the violence. This didn't sit well with Pablo. Carlos eventually had to go into hiding due to the extradition treaty with the U.S. When Carlos emerged from the jungle, Pablo considered him an enemy and rather than having Carlos assassinated, he told the Federalies where Carlos was hiding—resulting in his arrest and being sent immediately to the U.S.

Since Pablo's name and image were synonymous with violence, it was guilt by association for his partner Carlos, whom the prosecutors portrayed as a dangerous maniac.

Now, to defend my amigo Carlos' good name—I offer the following for your consideration. The Colombian security on Norman's Cay was there to protect us from any kidnapping plot the U.S. government might attempt. The Bahamian Government was being well paid to not interfere in our business, and we were always advised of any forthcoming jeopardy so that we could take necessary precautions. With this substantial protection and the fact that there was seldom any cash or drugs on the island, there was never any security need to block access to the island by air or sea. Even though the head of Carlos' security suggested the blocking of the runway—Carlos was adamant about making it available to anyone that wanted or needed to use it. This included other small smugglers that needed help to complete their trip. Carlos was courteous and generous to a fault to anyone that visited the island, unless you were affiliated in some way with the U.S. government.

The DEA tried several times to infiltrate the island, usually though the co-operation of ex-island residents. We knew almost immediately about the dual roles these James Bond wannabes (informants) were playing, but we considered them harmless because they represented no threat to us and snubbing them and cutting off their supplies soon made staying on the island a difficult prospect indeed. They all eventually moved on—with their cameras and notebooks—to more pleasant climes.

You must remember that our operation, as I previously described, was so organized, there was really nothing for anyone to see-, even if you were hanging out at the airport.

There was never any reason to murder any of these so-called known agents, much less innocent visitors that had enough nerve to visit our notorious (thanks to the rumor mill) island. I have never witnessed any violence on Norman's Cay, and I have spent more time on that island during our tenure there than ALL of the rest of the Americans put together.

It is my theory that these scoundrels (certain ex-island residents/informants who embellished or fabricated accounts of what took place on the island) were not law-abiding all American types who were interested in halting drug trafficking in the

Bahamas. On the contrary, our Bahamian staff was positive that a couple of these do-gooders were into some small -time hanky panky themselves. Our showing up on the island and taking control of it upset their leisurely lifestyle—and instead of becoming allies of ours—like four other friendly neighbors opted to do—they tried to intimidate us off by becoming informants for the Feds—hoping they could return the island to its original status—with them running it. Well, all of that treachery failed, but the name calling persisted due to authors believing these fantastic stories and publishing them as fact-, as most of the world now believes.

A note about our head of island security:

All of our security personnel were Colombians—headed up by a serious well-experienced man whose name I won't divulge—serving no particular purpose. We also had two Germans that were Morgan's personal body guards, accompanying him on visits to other islands—usually in one of his cigarette offshore race boats.

On three separate occasions I was with Morgan in meetings with the boss of his security force, where the boss tried to convince Carlos that assassination was the proper method of disposing of betrayers within the organization. One instance involved the wife of a friend of Morgan's from Colombia. She was a pretty thing and her past time was seducing any man on the island who was willing to risk the wrath of her husband. This created much dissention among the staff and the boss informed her that she must stop her promiscuity or suffer the consequences. Being a "Latin Spitfire", she went into a rage and threatened to contact the DEA and tell all, thus, the boss' request to Morgan to handle the situation the way that Pablo would—husband and wife at the bottom of the Bahamas trench.

Carlos was appalled by the idea, and with his usual cool demeanor told the boss that he, personally, would take care of the problem. He asked his friend to pack up and take his wife with him back to Colombia. Morgan gave him several thousand dollars, ordered up a jet to transport them, and reminded his friend and his wife that once they were in Colombia, he would be unable to rescue them if they misbehaved.

Another incident occurred when a sleazy American who Morgan met in a Colombian prison showed up on the island in a dilapidated sailboat, wife and child in hand, looking for a job. Morgan obliged, creating a position of trust for him doing odd jobs about the island. He made friends with a Bahamian that had a Cessna 172 aircraft on floats, and they were caught by the boss loading some kilos into the plane that had landed in the pond.

Infuriated, the boss had both of them in a boat ready to head out to sea—when Morgan and I arrived on the scene—having been informed of the incident. Morgan rescued the two scoundrels, commended the boss on a job well done, and informed the pilot of the float plane that if he ever returned to Norman's Cay, he would allow the boss to sink his plane where ever it was found.

The American sleaze was ordered to pack himself and his family up, and they were flown to Florida that very afternoon. Morgan gave him a kilo of coke in exchange for his sailboat, and advised him to sell it and use the money to start a new life, but that he was not welcome to return to Norman's Cay under any circumstances.

And finally, another incident involved Ed Ward's group—the Florida smuggling group that worked with us on the island—but fell out of favor with Morgan by letting greed overcome their common sense.

They became extremely belligerent and the boss begged Morgan to let him dispose of the whole group—providing a convincing story that if they were allowed to remain alive—they would come back to haunt us. Once again, Morgan refused to be involved in any violence and allowed the group to leave the island unharmed. Sadly, the boss' warning would come to pass, for they would eventually testify before the grand jury after being captured in Haiti and returned to the U.S. All of them would go Scott free after testifying against Morgan and me in the first trial.

CHAPTER THIRTY-SEVEN

THE ARRAIGNMENT AND A DENIAL OF CONSTITUTIONAL RIGHTS

B ACK IN THE Jacksonville courthouse, it was time for the arraignment. We were brought before a judge, the charges against us officially read, and asked how we pled. Morgan and I both pled "NOT GUILTY", and the trial date was set.

By this time, we both had attorneys. Mine was a young man from Jacksonville, appointed by the court, who turned out to be quite adept at law. Morgan, having substantial financial resources, hired two very well-known trial attorneys from South Florida. They rented an apartment in town, and flew home on the weekends.

Preparing for a trial of this magnitude is a long drawn out process, taking several months of pretrial hearings and developing a plan for our defense. The government and the defense teams are both obligated to furnish each other with the names of witnesses they intend to call, so that each side may prepare their strategy. However, adding to the list was a common procedure for the government during the trial proceedings. Introducing a new witness, without warning—prior to putting them on the stand to testify—was done frequently by the government with intense objections voiced by our attorneys, all of which were overruled by the judge. On the list that was made available to us, our investigators—who were hired by our attorneys—would research the background of the witnesses, frequently finding detrimental material allowing our attorneys to impeach (discredit) their testimony on cross examination.

Pretrial hearings were conducted by our attorneys, making motions before a Magistrate judge, who is a subordinate to the trial judge. These hearings were based on some type of misconduct by the government, requesting that the court alter or dismiss the charges brought against us prior to the onset of the trial. These motions are not heard by a jury. The Magistrate rules on these.

As an example: My first pretrial hearing was based on a motion to dismiss the charges against me, citing that I had been kidnapped by the government, and brought to the U.S. illegally, denying me my constitutional right to "Due Process". Due Process in this case would have been to petition the Panamanian government, which the U.S. has a treaty with, for "Extradition".

The hearing consisted of the DEA agent in charge of my abduction in Panama, being placed on the witness stand and questioned by my attorney about his complicity in my capture. He lied by testifying that the Panamanians conducted the raid, having filed charges against me. He testified that although he was indeed there, it was only as an observer and that he had no authority what-so-ever. When asked to produce a copy of the Panamanian charges against me, he testified to having misplaced them, but a copy was forthcoming. It never arrived. When questioned about how I happened to arrive in the U.S. aboard an aircraft confiscated by the DEA, which had departed Panama for a U.S. Air Force Base, and piloted by an American, he responded that it was an act of courtesy to the Panamanian government. An inquiry to that government by our investigator revealed that there were no charges against me, which he testified to during the hearing.

It was my turn to take the witness stand and tell my version. I described in great factual detail what I have already outlined at the beginning of this story, refuting the agent's testimony.

The testimony being completed, the prosecutor requested permission to address the court. Basically, he said that the government wasn't sure how the defendant arrived in the country. What we do know for sure is that he is here now, and you can be assured that we are going to prosecute him. It didn't take but a few minutes for the Magistrate to deny our motion. This set the precedent for the rest of our pretrial hearings.

The writing on the wall was becoming overwhelmingly obvious, and it became clear that our only hope depended on the courtroom skills of our attorneys and an impartial jury. The outcome of a trial often depends on the skills of the trial attorneys. Being found innocent hinges on the talents of the defendant's counsel. Knowledge of the law, of course, is absolutely necessary, but charisma and strategy are worth their weight in gold. A competent trial attorney is a specialist; lest we forget the famous drug trial of John DeLorean.

The next procedure is jury selection, which consists of twelve panelists of your peers. In anticipation of a lengthy trial, due to expected attrition, six alternate jurors were selected. The alternates would be seated with the regular jurors, so that they could replace any juror that had to be dismissed without interruption in the proceedings. During my first lengthy trial lasting eight months, there we indeed three jurors that had to be replaced; two due to health problems, and the other for misconduct in their private life.

These jurors are selected from several hundred that were randomly picked by a computer. They all resided in and around the Jacksonville area.

"Voir Dire" is a preliminary examination to determine the competence of each and every juror. In this particular trial, questioning was allowed by both the prosecutor and the defense counsel.

Leading questions ferreted out prejudiced jurors for both sides. It required a month of Voir Dire to finally select the eighteen panelists for the jury. All of the jurors admitted to having knowledge of who the defendants were and the circumstances surrounding the case, having been subjected to months of media publicity implemented by the prosecutor.

After the jury was selected, they were given instructions by the judge, who failed to mention-as previously pointed out. "jury nullification", which allows the jury to make decisions frowned upon by the court. They were told that they absolutely "could not" keep notes of the proceedings. They would be referred to by number instead of name, "for their protection", they were told. Also, for their safety, they would rendezvous at a secret location and be transported to the courthouse under the protection of the U.S. Marshalls. They would not be sequestered during the trial, but allowed to go home after their day in court with instructions to refrain from any exposure to media coverage of the trial, and with orders to not discuss the trial with anyone, including spouses and family. They would be questioned by the judge each day before the trial commenced, asking if they had complied with his orders. During the eight months of trial, not once did any juror admit to breaking the rules. We had an exceptionally honest and conscientious jury indeed!

During the entire time I was in custody, Sheldon was there to assist me. She frequently visited me in the county jail where I was detained, and assisted my and Morgan's counsel by furnishing them with information about any of the government's witnesses that she was aware of. During the preparation of our defense, Sheldon was invited to stay with my attorney and his wife. She never missed one day of any courtroom proceedings, including the entire trial. A true friend indeed, especially since she had acquired a new boyfriend. My feelings were hurt, but Sheldon's happiness and well-being meant the world to me, so I was able to accept this, knowing she must move on and build a new life without me.

By the time jury selection had started, a holding facility had been constructed in the courthouse. It was a few doors from the courtroom where we were being tried. This was where Morgan was held for the duration of the trial. Very tight security prevailed on this floor of the building with additional Marshalls being assigned and rotated every week or two. They arrived from all over the country for their tour of duty.

The Marshals would pick me up at the county jail very early in the morning and dress me out in my court clothes. Sheldon kept these furnished and clean for me. I was then chained up and transported the thirty miles to court. There were often media camera men waiting near the courthouse parking area trying to get a shot for the day's news. Once inside and secure in the Marshall's holding tank, my shackles were removed. I was eventually re-chained and escorted upstairs to Morgan's stockade where we were free to enjoy each other's company, reminisce about old times, discuss the case, and the frequent mail Carlos received from admirer's through-out the trial. Some of these fans were a little eccentric. I had a few, but Morgan had the lion's share; with his most notable pen pal being the famed television news anchor woman Diane Sawyer who corresponded with Morgan on a regular basis. Morgan's quarters, the Marshal's holding tank, and the courtroom itself, were the only places where we weren't restrained with some type of bondage. During lunch break, we were taken to a secure room located on the roof of building where the SWAT team was located. Even with several Marshal in the room, we were shackled to the leg of the chair we occupied with an ankle cuff while we ate our lunch.

Frequently, before and after the day in court, our attorneys would be escorted to Morgan's stockade where we could privately discuss our strategy.

It was discovered by our counsel that Marshals with concealed weapons in small canvas bags were seated in the back of the courtroom while the trial was in progress. On the premise of jury intimidation, our counsel requested that they be removed. This was one of the few motions granted.

During jury selection, Morgan's attorneys hired psychologists specializing in the recognition of traits that might qualify a person to be a beneficial or adverse juror. Anyone who was obviously prejudiced and wasn't dismissed by the judge could be summarily dismissed by the government or the defense. Each side was allowed eight strikes (options) to do so without any explanation.

Most of the prospective jurors questioned indicated that they were neutral in their opinions. But there were more than a few that were outspoken about any person suspected of dealing drugs. Conversely, there was one gentleman who was a professor of constitutional law, who very eloquently made it quite clear to the court that, the defendants in this, or any other Federal drug

case, were being held illegally—and should be released immediately. Unfortunately, he wasn't aware that the court no longer
dealt with constitutional law. He was thanked for his opinion
and dismissed by the judge.

The final jury consisted of eight women and four men; the
foreman of the jury being male. The alternate jurors, if my
memory serves me correctly, were all women. I was pleased that
the majority of the jury was female, knowing that Morgan's
charisma and good looks would be valuable assets.

It was a gala event the day the trial commenced. The courtroom
was packed; priority seating going first to security, then friends of
the court, media artists, and finally, what few seats were left, went
to spectators. If it had been a play on Broadway, it would have
been a huge success. S.R.O.!

CHAPTER THIRTY-EIGHT

LONGEST RUNNING DRUG TRIAL IN U.S. HISTORY: OPENING ARGUMENTS AND OTHER ABSURDITIES

THE TRIAL COMMENCES. After a preliminary discourse by the judge, the first order of business is opening arguments. An allotted amount of time is given to each side. This is to lay the groundwork to the jury, describing their version of the case and what they plan to prove or disprove. Morgan's attorneys traded off on addressing the jury and cross examination. "Cross" is our counsel's opportunity to question the government's witnesses after they have testified on direct examination for the government. This is a very dramatic part of the trial, both sides attempting to convince the jury of their theory. This is sometimes done with great emotion, and acting ability would be a considerable asset.

As the accuser, the government presents their case to the jury first, calling as many witnesses as they think are necessary. The defense has the option to cross examine the government's witnesses. Of the more than one hundred witnesses the government put on the stand, less than half were actual finger pointers. These were the ones that our attorneys attacked on cross examination.

Cross is the critical part of the trial, requiring great skill, attempting to discredit the testimony of the government witnesses. Indeed, as it turned out, many of the major witnesses for the government had their testimony impeached (discredited), or the witnesses' character was proven to be tainted; admitting to being bribed by the government for their cooperation and testimony.

The remaining government witnesses were giving corroborating testimony regarding Morgan's business deals. This included his banking records, aircraft purchases and sales, etc. These witnesses required little or no cross examination.

The trial was fascinating, resembling the classic Perry Mason television series. The entire eight month proceeding was so involved my attorney had to install four book shelves in his office, each four feet in length, just to hold the typed trial transcripts. He estimated that there were about fifty thousand pages in all.

A few highlights worth mentioning include the first witness for the government. He was a smuggler named George Jung. He is the central character portrayed by actor Johnny Depp in the popular 2001 motion picture "Blow", in which parts of this story are depicted. Jung testified against Morgan, whose name in the movie is "Diego", regarding his part in the beginning of the cocaine smuggling conspiracy. Jung's testimony was given for considerable leniency from the government.

Most of the Jacksonville smuggling group, led by Ed, who had visited Sheldon and me in Canada, were put on the stand. One in particular was in the process of giving testimony regarding what had taken place on the island in meetings the group had with Morgan. Running out of time, his testimony was put on hold until the court reconvened at a later date. When the trial was restarted, he became extremely hostile towards the prosecutor on direct examination. He was dismissed by the government; and it was our turn to cross examine. He had no reservations testifying that the prosecutor had "double-crossed" him. He told the story of having left a hundred thousand dollars in cash hidden on the island. For his co-operation with the government, among other perks, he was told he would be allowed to bring his money to the U.S. —no questions asked—and not subject to any taxes. Which he did. Apparently, the IRS didn't know about the deal, and they paid him a visit demanding their pound of flesh. On the stand, he testified that he was finished lying for the prosecutor, stating that most of his testimony had been prompted, and his deal with government was done. The prosecutor was livid, recalling the witness to the stand, where he attempted to discredit him and his story. I can only offer an educated guess as to what happened to this poor soul.

About midway through the trial, a prisoner was placed in the county jail where I was being held. He was a distinguished well educated man, who had been accused of perpetrating some fraud against the government. When he discovered who I was, he informed me that he personally knew our prosecutor and judge very well. He offered to testify in our behalf about a conspiracy that he was aware of, that had happened years before. It involved our judge and several other prominent people. He had copies of documents sent in confirming what he had told me, and said that he was capable of proving, without a doubt, the conspiracy that he described. I shared all of this information with Morgan, and we presented it to our attorneys during our next meeting. They were appalled to hear this and refused to discuss it any further, which came as a surprise to Morgan and me. We discussed it between the two of us and decided to proceed on our own.

I had enough copies of the documents made to distribute to the judge and the prosecutor and delivered them to Morgan.

He wanted to personally bring the matter up in court. Midway through the next day's trial, Morgan stood up and asked for permission to make a statement, which was granted. He told the judge he had information and documentation that implicated him in a conspiracy that the prosecutor had inadvertently discovered—and has subsequently been coercing the judge to have his way in court.

A dead silence fell over the courtroom. When the judge regained his composure, he ordered the jury dismissed and cleared the room. This was big news for the media which played it up in the news that night: "Lehder accuses prosecutor of blackmailing judge!"

Morgan passed the documents to the judge and the prosecutor; the prosecutor immediately recognizing the papers and the informant. With a flushed face bulging blood vessels, he went into a rage accusing the informant of having a personal grudge against him with there being no basis for the accusation.

The judge maintained enough composure to tell Morgan that when the court convened the following day, he expected a formal complaint to be filed.

We were escorted to Morgan's stockade and our attorneys soon followed. They were discouraged about the whole affair. After being scolded that "now we've done it"—we asked for an explanation as to why they hadn't proceeded when it was first brought to their attention. After all, if it was indeed true, as the documents indicated, then we were being tried in a "Kangaroo Court"—with the deck stacked against us. Neither of our counsel could refute that statement. Without them saying so, it appeared that their intervention into this matter was some type of professional "no no" that they didn't wish to discuss. However, they did mention that the procedure now is for the judge to recuse (dismiss) himself and with a new judge appointed, a mistrial would be declared. We would have to start over.

Morgan and I had a private discussion regarding this new information and agreed that starting over was not in our best interest, especially since we had done so well discrediting the government's witnesses thus far. We decided it would be prudent to drop the issue, and notified our counsel of our decision. They were relieved and agreed it was a good idea; that we were indeed looking very strong in our defense.

The next morning, the court convened as usual. The judge made no reference to what had transpired just hours before. He directed the prosecutor to call his next witness. No mention was ever made again of the incident, not even the media had any comment. I mentioned to Morgan a day later that maybe we just shared a daydream where only he and I were involved. A very strange set of circumstances indeed!

CHAPTER THIRTY-NINE

WALTER CRONKITE TAKES THE STAND

The prosecutor notified us in court one morning that he would be calling renowned TV news anchorman Walter Cronkite as a witness. We were surprised to hear this and correctly surmised that the prosecutor had discovered that Walter had visited Norman's Cay on his sailboat to visit our mutual friend Ray, the island's oldest resident. This would not have been the first time that Walter had done this, and he was not the only dignitary that visited Ray.

Because of Walter being a notable person, it was unlikely he would be treated like a regular witness, being interrogated prior to being placed on the witness stand. We speculated that the prosecutor was on a "fishing trip,", hoping to coax Walter into giving some type of incriminating testimony about the island and its unsavory occupants. We were correct in our assumption. When the prosecutor asked Walter to explain the circumstances of his visit to Norman's Cay, Walter testified that he had been cruising the Bahamas on vacation as he did almost every year. It was his custom to stop by Norman's Cay to see if his old friend

Ray was on the island. He anchored offshore and rowed his dinghy to Norman's dock. There he was met by a Bahamian employee of Morgan's. He testified that he was treated cordially and was told that Ray was not presently on the island. Upon inquiry, he was informed that the island was now owned by Morgan and the hotel and bar were closed for remodeling.

Walter also testified that he was invited to use the island's guest facilities if he pleased, but the employee made it clear the island was basically closed to tourists. Having no reason to stay, Walter declined the offer and sailed on to another destination.

Upon further questioning by the prosecutor, Walter denied receiving any threatening treatment, seeing any type of weapon, nor did he see any Colombian security personnel. He said that he was pleased to learn that the young Colombian owner was returning the island and its facilities to its former condition. He said that he considered Norman's Cay to be one of the most beautiful islands in the Bahamas, and one of his favorites.

On a very brief cross examination, he testified that he was aware of several privately owned islands in the Bahamas where it was the custom to receive permission to come ashore, as it was with any other private property that he was aware of. The prosecutor went fishing, and never got a nibble.

On another day, having no physical evidence of drugs to present to the jury, the perceptive prosecutor decided to improvise. From a police warehouse containing confiscated drugs, he had a cart containing kilos of cocaine wheeled into the courthouse. He got permission from the judge to have it placed right in front of the jury where it could be clearly seen. Its unique odor could be detected from anywhere in the courtroom. We objected, but it was over-ruled. This ploy was used for several days running while the prosecutor boldly attempted to convince the jury that this product was somehow connected to our Norman's Cay operation. The only witnesses were government agents. When questioned by the prosecutor, they gave shrewdly devised answers that would tend to incriminate our island group. With great cunning on the part of our counsel, cross examination of the government agents revealed that the drugs actually came from an unrelated group that was already in prison. Their method of importation, it was discovered, was shipping the product into ports on the eEast Coast in hollowed out logs destined for a lumber mill. A valiant but unsuccessful attempt by our overzealous opponent.

A unique scheme by our counsel was to wheel a large blackboard into the courtroom to keep a running account of information derived from government witnesses on cross examination. As information was accumulated regarding rewards paid, taxes/fines/restitutions and sentences dismissed or reduced, it was entered on the blackboard. Subtotals were calculated for the jury to see. It was shown that these very impressive totals were for deals made with the government for the witnesses' cooperation and testimony.

All but a couple of friends and acquaintances that visited Norman's Cay ended up on the witness stand for the government. There were many more that have not been mentioned. Also, there were a few that showed up and testified, claiming that they were associates of Morgan or myself, that neither one of us had ever seen before. I won't speculate as to how that happened.

It should be mentioned that the banks in the Bahamas, except for the Swiss banks, cannot be trusted to maintain their "secrecy" laws for any type of transaction. This was readily demonstrated in our trial when a small contingency from Nassau showed up in court quite eager to testify with all of Morgan's banking records.

For reasons, that to this day I don't understand, our attorneys decided to relinquish our option to present a defense. Even though we had presented an extensive witness list to the government, the moment that the government declared that it was resting its case, our counsel did likewise. This decision came as a surprise to everyone that appeared to be greatly disappointed that Morgan and I didn't get a chance to testify in our behalf. I speculate that our counsel feared the skills of the prosecutor when he would have the opportunity to question us on cross examination.

CHAPTER FORTY

THE VERDICT

ALL OF THE evidence had been presented to the jury. Closing arguments came next, with the government presenting their argument first. The defense followed with the government given a second opportunity to contradict the defense argument. A bit unreasonable it would seem!

It must be remembered that for eight months, the jury listened to well over one hundred witnesses giving testimony. They were denied the opportunity to take notes, trusting a vast amount of information to memory. That would leave closing arguments very influential in the jury's judgment, relying more on the talents of the debater, than the facts and personalities exhibited by the witnesses.

A very strange turn of events occurred about this time. Our enthusiastic prosecutor never got to taste the victory that he worked so diligently for. Prior to the jury returning their verdict, the prosecutor resigned his position as the U.S. Attorney for the Middle District of Florida. His assistant finished the final loose ends of the trial.

Rumors were rife regarding this unexpected incident. One can only surmise that for him to give up his life-long ambitions when he had his foot in the door was that he possibly fell out of favor with those in higher authority. The last I heard of him, he was going into private practice as a defense attorney. *(MayCay Beeler's notes: Robert W. Merkle, Jr., nicknamed "Mad Dog" for his pugnacious prosecuting style, resigned his position in the Federal Prosecutor's post to make an unsuccessful run for the U.S. Senate. He was in private practice until his death in 2003.)*

The next procedure in the trial was for the jury to receive their instructions from the judge. This was lengthy and somewhat complicated. He briefly mentioned "reasonable doubt" but not one word about their great authority endowed by the Constitution.

The jury was dismissed to deliberate. They were sequestered in a hotel by the Marshals where they were isolated from any source of influence. It took them one week to decide that we were guilty on all counts. Morgan and I were brought to court the next day where the verdict was read to us by the judge. A very solemn ritual!

We were returned shortly thereafter for sentencing, which resulted in the maximum allowed by law, which I mentioned earlier. Morgan and I embraced each other before going our separate ways. We have not seen each other since.

CHAPTER FORTY-ONE

APPEALS

SEPARATELY, **OUR ATTORNEYS** filed appeals for us in the Circuit Court. This higher court reviews alleged discrepancies of law that the defendant claims the lower court made during the trial. Frequently, relief is given in this court; however, knowing how to weave your way through the system is a prerequisite. Morgan's appeal was very lengthy, and prepared by one of the most highly regarded post-conviction attorneys in the country. It complained of a long series of infractions that were made before and during the trial. My appeal was less elaborate, adopting much of Morgan's argument. Both of our appeals fell on deaf ears in the higher court and were denied.

By law, we were allowed to take our grievances to the Supreme Court. This court grants hearings to less than two percent of the motions sent to them, usually settling conflicting issues between the lower courts. Seldom does a motion of our status receive a hearing. We were advised to drop it.

Morgan was designated to return to the maximum security prison to serve his sentence. I was sent to the Atlanta prison in Georgia which had been reopened after mass destruction by Cuban rioters. I was there for a few months when a staff member read a story in a prominent magazine about our trial and where we had been sent. For reasons of security, I was then sent to the Federal Correctional Institution in Memphis, Tennessee. I have been here at that location since 1989.

Friends have come and gone, mostly gone. Sheldon remained in touch with me, as has my dear sister, Phyrne, while others cut all ties. After being coerced and blackmailed by prosecutors in both trials to testify against Morgan and me, our close friends and associates completely abandoned us. I could tell that it was very difficult for them to condemn us on the witness stand—with no eye contact and obvious tears—as they unveiled the story the government rehearsed them to say for several weeks prior to their testimony. I felt a deep sympathy for them—having been placed in the position of having to choose between Morgan and me—and the threat of the involvement of their immediate families—i.e., as previously mentioned, Dyan was threatened with a draconian prison sentence and having her four -year old son placed in a foster home. For her cooperation with the government she was rewarded with probation for basically being a friend of Morgan and me. These Feds play some extreme 'hard ball'!

CHAPTER FORTY-TWO

ANOTHER INDICTMENT– ROUND TWO

I HAD BEEN IN Memphis less than a year when prosecutor Ernst Mueller, who had finished the trial in Jacksonville (after the U.S. Attorney resigned), filed another indictment against me. This one charged me with another conspiracy, officially called "Continuing Criminal Enterprise", and being a "Kingpin". The government failed to include these charges in the first indictment, even though they had had all of the information. The conspiracy charge on this indictment was for distribution; the first trial conspiracy having been for smuggling.

I was temporarily returned to Jacksonville, and during the year that I was there, I was moved around to various county jails, some resembling dungeons. It was tough to endure; along with the "diesel therapy" in which I was bused all over God's green earth in an unsuccessful effort to break me; to make me talk. It was all a bit much. I presumed this shabby treatment was the result of my once again refusing to cooperate with the government; because yet again, I refused to rat on my dear amigo Morgan, or divulge information about other players including Manuel

Noriega. I am many things, but I'm no God damn rat! You may think I'm a fool for holding my tongue; for not saving myself (like everyone else did!) by taking advantage of the prosecutor's promises of reduced sentences in exchange for snitching on associates. I never once entertained that proposal. Not once! That was never a consideration for me. I'm no God damn rat!

Since my first conviction, there had been legislation enacted changing the sentencing guidelines. By going to trial on these new charges, I was looking at a possible "Natural Life" sentence on both counts if I was found guilty. A little severe I thought, in as much as there had not been any evidence or a victim of my crimes.

The indictment contained four co-defendants; only one I that was vaguely familiar with. In a conspiracy, it isn't necessary that you know all of the co-conspirators, or their particular criminal acts. All conspirators are responsible for each other's actions. This is the trial where the court initially mistakenly appointed me the real estate attorney mentioned earlier. Unreal!

There was a different judge for this trial. He rarely showed-up in court in good humor. He explained to the jury prior to the trial commencing that if they noticed him nodding off, it was because he had just had back surgery and was heavily medicated. WHAT? I found this statement interesting. Also of interest to me, and apparently no one else, was when the judge admonished the prosecutor in open court for pursuing this indictment in the first place. Being totally familiar with the first trial, he told the prosecutor that he was wasting the court's valuable time and "that they both know that this new indictment would never fly". He recessed the court for thirty minutes to decide if he was going to continue. Upon returning, his decision was to let the prosecutor continue and "let the Eleventh Circuit Court of Appeals take care of the problem". I imagined the Eleventh Circuit

Court would be pleased to hear this bit of news. Having had the experience of the previous trial, I could plainly see the writing on the wall, and it wasn't pretty.

Jury selection took one day for this trial, with the judge conducting the Voir Dire. Counsel for the defendants was not allowed to participate. One prospective juror, when questioned by the judge, adamantly stated that she was prejudiced against anyone who dealt in drugs; her son having had an unfortunate experience. The judge sympathized with her, and declared, in open court, that if he had his way, he "would hang every drug dealer". He told the juror that he felt that she was capable of making a reasonable decision as to our innocence or guilt, and kept her on as a juror.

I decided that as long as I was going to be "railroaded", I might as well do it in comfort. I wore jeans, a sweatshirt and sneakers for the duration of the trial. And, yes, the judge found this irritating. Having had twenty years to reflect and meditate on this, I now realize what a fool I had been. At the time I was convinced that any efforts to save myself were futile. Having since evolved through metaphysical studies, I now concede that this defeatist attitude was a big mistake. I have since learned to take full responsibility for my actions. As certain as I was that I had no chance, I was rewarded with exactly what I expected. I create my own reality and am presently striving to master this philosophy.

With only a few exceptions, the witnesses for the government were the best witnesses from the first trial. I knew almost verbatim what their testimony would be, and coached my attorney on the proper cross examination. Unfortunately, his expertise was not in courtroom procedure, and it was to no avail.

I couldn't see wasting any more time attempting to put on a defense, and declined to testify. We rested our case, much to my attorney's delight.

The trial lasted six weeks. The jury returned their verdict in a few hours, having been escorted to a private room in the court house to deliberate.

Three of us were found guilty. Two were acquitted, having put on a worthy defense with tales of heroism by one defendant and persuasive weeping by the other.

As I expected, I received the two natural life sentences—running consecutive—which means that when I die after serving the first sentence, I am obligated to start the other. I never could figure out how that worked. For good measure, the judge gave me a two million dollar fine; this, after having a hearing before the onset of the trial to determine if I had any assets to hire an attorney of my choice. It was determined that I was a pauper.

A few years ago, I received a notice from the government accounting office reminding me that they had not received any payment on my two million dollar court-imposed fine. With accrued interest, the balance was now approaching four million dollars. I was given thirty days to pay my outstanding debt in full, or further action would be taken. I saved the notice for future amusement.

CHAPTER FORTY-THREE

WHAT HAPPENED TO?

AFTER I WAS sent to prison on the first trial, Sheldon remained in Jacksonville and attempted to develop a new lifestyle in the establishment. When I returned for my second trial, she visited me often and was once again in the courtroom for every proceeding.

Eventually, Sheldon moved back to the West Coast, but none of it compared to the years of adventure that we had shared. She purchased a small boat and sailed it to the Bahamas, where she tried to re-establish her island lifestyle by moving back into our abandoned beach bungalow on Norman's Cay. She reconditioned it and lived there for many years with her boyfriend; however, it was never the same as it was when Morgan and I were there. Sheldon ultimately moved back to Panama, purchasing different property where she and her boyfriend built a new house; our one-time cozy homestead on the blue lagoon having been ransacked by our native neighbors that salvaged what they could for their personal use. Much better they found a use for it than letting the steaming tropical jungle reclaim it, which would have happened in short order.

I had long worried and wondered what had become of our beloved canine Norman who had been left behind to fend for himself after we were apprehended in Panama. Sheldon told me she had indeed learned of his fate, but felt it was in my best interest not to disclose the details.

After many years of staying in contact with one another, it was Sheldon's desire to cut off all communication with me, citing that I was a hard act for her boyfriend to follow. Out of respect and love for my best friend, who needed to move her life forward without my interference, I complied with Sheldon's wishes. I shall always have fond memories of this exceptional lady, for we shared a great adventure and much happiness.

As for Sheldon's mom, she corresponded with me in prison after Sheldon was out of my life. I had long sensed this woman's affection for me—which I never returned—having absolutely no interest, and can only surmise that may have triggered her Jekyll and Hyde behavior toward me. My preferring her daughter over her was a sore spot and likely the root of her hatred toward me. Mom did express some remorse for unknowingly (?) leading the DEA to my Panamanian paradise; as well as the previous fiascos she instigated by flat out lying to the FBI, claiming I had kidnapped and raped her daughter at gunpoint; and that subsequent incident in which she called the cops on me, turning me in for pot possession after she had eagerly shared a joint with me in my apartment.

I accepted her claims of this so-called remorse until a mutual acquaintance informed me that at the very same time of her friendly correspondence, Mom was spreading rumors on the outside declaring what a monster I was; ranting on and on about how I had brutally raped and kidnapped her daughter. The same old lie, the same old story. And that did it. I had finally had enough and put an end to our communication for good. I destroyed her correspondence. When I didn't reply to her further missives, she eventually stopped writing. Thank God! Enough is enough. What a fool I had been to keep giving this temperamental woman the benefit of the doubt all those years. Enough already! Lesson learned. Believe who people are when they show you the first time. Imagine the grief this may have spared me had I learned it early on.

"Put your ear down close to your soul, and listen hard."
–Anne Sexton

CHAPTER FORTY-FOUR

PARADISE TO PRISON LIFE

"WAREHOUSING OF SOULS" is how I best define prison. The system has become so overcrowded, and there is no longer rehabilitation.

The Memphis Federal Correctional Institution is a far cry from the cozy home I left behind in Panama. Old and dilapidated, it used to be a juvenile detention home or something along those lines before the Bureau of Prisons took it over. Crumbling cement, splintering and warped wood on window frames exude a forlorn ambiance. Multicolored paint peeling through, exposing layers like strata in the earth, a silent testimony of the long forgotten prisoners who have come and gone. Old tiles, marred by gouges, haphazardly placed along communal pathways. The feeling is always mercurial depending on the time of day or intramural happenings. Drama between the fellas, born of boredom over petty differences or a muted excitement because of some rumored change in the law. Frantic activity on the verge of panic when a horde of officers descend on the unit to do a mass search for contraband. The anger and despair of knowing your carefully arranged cell and two man closet/bathroom were about to be violated and ravaged by an uncaring staff member. The prison is two floors of institutional architecture refurbished as the security requirements necessitated. Boarded up skylights, bars welded over patio windows.

I rise early at five am. Our cells are unlocked at five-thirty on weekdays, six forty-five on weekends. I shower, then weather permitting, sit on a certain bench every morning after my walk around the track. I watch the pair of hawks that live on the power line trail behind the prison. As an elder and long-time exemplary prisoner, I am afforded this luxury by my keepers who allow me to sit, drink my coffee, and watch the sun rise. I contemplate whether I will spend the morning painting or working on my latest brief in the prison law library. I lament the loss of the glorious big trees that graced the prison yard until one particularly hated warden cut them all down. Hundred year old oaks. Unbelievable. I cruise around in shorts and a t-shirt and whatever tennis shoes I happen to have bought that are still wearable. I am saving a brand new pair of shoes and sweats for my release day. Even though my sentence demands life in prison, with the intention I will die here, my faith believes otherwise. I *will* earn my freedom! This I *know*—somehow, someway, some day.

Lunch is served in the cafeteria from ten-thirty 'til noon to groups on a rotation plan. My typical diet here is garbage; almost any type of bean, rice and potatoes are my favorites when available. I don't eat flesh, not since my days in Panama when I acquired a deep love and respect for nature's creatures.

After lunch, I nap. My advanced age and status as a model inmate during my tenure here allow advantages that make life a little easier. Afterwards, depending on the day, I tend to my work duties as a clerk for my unit counselor. At four PM there is an institutional count. The evening meal commences at five, feeding twelve-hundred of us. My evening activities consist of an hour or two in the library socializing, writing, typing or reading; or spending time out in the recreation yard hanging out. Everything closes at eight PM, when we are confined in our units to watch TV, use the phone, or cook snacks in the microwave. That shuts down at ten, when we are secured in our cells for the rest of the night. My particular unit—Delta B—holds bed space for one hundred and twenty-nine souls. I am usually ready to rest my eyes and turn-in around eight.

Day to day boredom prevails. Because of this, one of my favorite past times is sleeping—averaging ten to twelve hours a day—which is way more than I would like to report.

I never watch TV except for an occasional NASCAR race— and I'm losing interest in that; it having become more of a show biz spectacle than a contest of skill.

I am constantly surrounded by people in an environment that precludes the luxury of privacy; thus, there is never a moment that can be depended on to provide a guarantee of no intrusion into my life. This is torture in itself. And the noise—the incessant noise—it wears you down except for the few hours at night when we are secured in our rooms (earplugs help). I feel like a peaceful dove confined to a cage. Clipped wings; in hibernation; feeling helpless. The harsh reality is we are warehoused like feedlot cattle waiting hopefully for a light at the end of a tunnel that isn't an oncoming train. God, it's difficult being surrounded by so much negative counter-productive energy! Melancholy sets in. I would give anything to be able to view my confinement as a thing of joy. I would certainly settle for a continual positive attitude, but I have faltered at this elusive goal. I have read, studied, and contemplated everything that held my slightest interest, looking for solutions. I'm hanging in there.

My salvation lies in my spiritual, philosophical and home-steading studies; the joy of my creative endeavors (painting and writing); eating; sleeping; and most of all, the hope of eventual freedom.

My cell is constructed of cold concrete block. It is typical with two bunks in an 8 x 15 foot room complete with two lockers, a small desk, combo sink and toilet. There are two small windows—one with an outside view, the other in the steel door facing the common area where the TVs are located. There are no old-fashioned bars.

My current cellie is a Mexican chap who has been my guest for several months. When I say "guest", it is because I have extreme seniority (I have been here in Memphis since 1989—except for a one year trip back to Jacksonville for my second trial) and our room is considered mine. I make it quite clear to new guests that our cell is to be considered a sanctuary—a place we rest and are isolated as much as possible from the horde. This precludes having visitors and any other intrusion into our/my precious privacy.

It doesn't take my roommates long to find out that I have no interest in being their friend; that's because we have nothing in common to discuss—except prison—and I have little patience with that topic. In fact, because I am an anti-establishment expatriate, I have little in common with any of my fellow in-mates—except that we are all considered criminals; therefore, by choice, I spend much of my time by myself. I have become more or less oblivious to time, and might be considered in a state of semi-dormancy.

I have an old school spring mattress that I cherish since it is one of the last of its kind for five states in any direction. It's topped off with some foam business I acquired that resembles packing material. This is one indulgence I enjoy; while others, I decline. Weed is readily available here, yet I deny it. The pot that had brought me so much pleasure on the outside is not worth the high behind bars considering the consequences of being caught with contraband. Yes, I miss it. I smoked it a few times when I first got to prison, but quickly disciplined myself to forego it. Not worth it, and my status as a seasoned exemplary prisoner has been the reward.

Over the years, I have learned that the easiest way to do this time is to ignore my foolish pride and allow myself to become institutionalized—which means follow the rules. Life becomes much easier.

While I pass on pot, there are other pleasantries I enjoy. I savor certain neat little gadgets that the other guys have made for me over the years; like a super high tech stinger (water heater) I can drop into my coffee to heat it up so I don't have to venture downstairs and deal with the unsavory types first thing in the morning. Little things like that start to dig at you after years of it. Knowing that most every guy you encounter that pisses you off will be out of prison before you, to the detriment of society. A total waste of freedom. You think about that while your coffee heats up...I'm telling you.

CHAPTER FORTY-FIVE

I'M NO GODDAMN RAT

AFTER THE SECOND sentencing, my trial counsel filed an appeal on my behalf. He succeeded in convincing the Court of Appeals that my Kingpin charge had violated the Double Jeopardy clause of the Constitution (Double Jeopardy is a procedural defense that forbids a defendant from being tried again on the same or similar charges following a legitimate acquittal or conviction). Having no recourse for this situation, my Kingpin sentence was reversed and vacated by the higher court. This left me with one life sentence on the conspiracy charge.

A moment's reflection on the preceding information is in order: A prudent person would likely assume that the U.S. Attorney's office—which includes their clerks, legal research department, and prosecutors—would be knowledgeable of the basic fundamentals of law. They likely have the latest technology and information to competently research an indictment before presenting it to a grand jury. Thus, it seems unlikely that a major

Constitutional violation, like Double Jeopardy, would elude their scrutiny when they constructed my second indictment.

The same theory could apply to the court when they tested, or should have tested, the indictment's accuracy. It was so blatant that the trial judge recognized it and warned the prosecutor as I discussed earlier. I am puzzled as to why my counsel didn't bring this conspicuous error to the attention of the court at the onset of the trial, instead of waiting to present it on my direct appeal.

The fact remains that the higher court reversed and vacated the conviction. No one said it, but it seems obvious that what was in error in the higher court had to be in error at its conception. One has to ponder if this represents the quality of our judicial system, or if other factors were involved.

The reason I am enduring this draconian sentence is because I refused to co-operate with the government, plain and simple. I refused to rat.

To recap, I have participated in two trials. In my first, it was only Carlos and me. I was charged with and found guilty of a conspiracy to import cocaine (smuggling). I was given a fifteen -year sentence.

The government discovered that there were several V.I.P.'s involved in our conspiracy, and because Carlos couldn't be indicted twice for crimes that he had been found guilty of in the first trial, I was re-indicted, this time charged with RING LEADER status and CONSPIRACY TO DISTRIBUTE the same cocaine that I had transported. The government was hoping that these additional charges would coerce me to finally co-operate with them, spill the beans, and divulge information concerning the previously mentioned V.I.P.'s. When I once again refused, they took me to trial again, in what is referred to as a "Kangaroo Court". They broke many of their own laws to convict me and left me to overcome their devious work through post-conviction litigation, which I have been pursuing for two decades.

The second trial produced TWO life sentences (for a non-violent offender!), both of which were illegal. Thus far, I have managed to have one of the sentences reversed and vacated by a higher court. My remaining life sentence is as illegal as the vacated sentence, and I keep one or two motions in court at all times, with the help of other inmates that are more knowledge-able about law than I. The mockery of justice does not end in the trial courts—it is rife throughout the entire judicial system and could basically be referred to as a dog and pony show.

However, the law books in our prison library indicate that there are several, including my sentence that was overturned, that do get relief from the courts; therefore, it is possible, and I keep searching for that special argument that will convince the court to vacate my existing illegal sentence.

What I was actually guilty of was the importation (smuggling) charge, which would have consisted of an eight -and -a half -year sentence, with a "good time" reduction (I am an exemplary inmate). I have now exceeded twenty-one years.

The courts are not the only hope on the horizon. Laws are constantly being reconsidered by Congress that could be ben-eficial to me. There is a bill presently being considered by the Senate which has already been unanimously passed by the House of Representatives and appears that it will be enacted into law. It is called the SECOND CHANCE bill, and without going into boring details, it contains a supplement that I refer to as the OLD GEEZER bill. The way it is written today, it would include me as a potential candidate. It stipulates that if you are over sixty and have been incarcerated for half of your sentence, or more than ten years, and have never been convicted of a violent crime, you are eligible for release. I qualify!

Then, there is much attention being given to reinstating parole, which I would qualify for if it was re-established as it was when it was discontinued in 1987.

Thus, there is reason for hope, but unfortunately, as I write this, it is not possible to place a time on any of the above. I rely heavily on my intuition. It keeps reassuring me that as long as I have FAITH in my freedom and happiness, I will attain these goals. So far, my intuition has an excellent track record, and I do have the FAITH.

For several years, I just accepted the face value of my situation. A fellow inmate who was knowledgeable about law and was familiar with my case told me that he believed he could help me gain my freedom. He seemed positive that there had been a major error made by the trial court regarding my conspiracy conviction. Upon examination of the proceedings and the laws in effect, it turned out that there had been more than one error made. My friend wrote a motion. The government responded with their argument. I had a time limit to respond. For failing to pass a drug test, my friend was placed in isolation and eventually shipped to another prison. I desperately found another person who claimed to be experienced at law to assist me. Unfortunately, his response was inadequate, and my motion was denied. I was to discover later that recent laws had been enacted to allow only one attempt to challenge a mistake, and I had carelessly used mine.

I spent much time in our prison law library attempting to learn how to research the complicated procedures of law, hoping to glean enough information to save myself. I didn't want to be dependent on someone else who may be here today and gone tomorrow. Reaching a point where I felt fairly confident that

I could write a motion that would circumvent the problem of being blocked for rearguing my issue, I gave it a try. That attempt failed also. And so it has gone over the years. New knowledgeable friends, new attempts on my behalf, and new failures. Everyone agrees that I have excellent issues for being released. It seems that the government has a technical procedure for blocking every attempt without having to address the issues I have presented.

A bit over a year ago, an inmate by the name of Gary, who has been incarcerated for thirty-five years, was transferred to this institution. His constant pursuit and understanding of law for those many years has given him a win record that would be envied by licensed attorneys in the free world. Gary has taken an interest in my situation and is presently assisting me. He feels confident that he will overcome my problems and that I will be free in the near future. Needless to say, I am excited with this new prospect.

Today is the 8th day of August, 2005. Because I have no intention of doing anything with what I have written, the story is finished. When the day comes that I win my freedom, depending on the circumstances at that time, I may, or may not write an epilog and publish my story.

Suffice it to say that I have accomplished my purpose for writing my story, for it has exceeded my expectations for reliving the adventure that Sheldon and I shared for those many years. Now it is time to return to my legal work.

A TWIST OF FATE

"Never give up, for that is just the place and time that the tide will turn." —Harriett Beecher Stowe

TODAY IS THE 3rd day of February, 2013. With a heavy heart, I write Jack's epilogue in his absence.

About two years after Jack wrote that last chapter, a significant shift occurred that would change everything.

That's when I contacted Jack in prison at the Federal Correctional Institution in Memphis for research on a documentary I was producing about Norman's Cay. As mentioned in my addendum to Jack's introduction in this book, initially, Jack wasn't interested. After two decades in prison, he was sick and tired of media hounding him for the infamous story of his conviction in the longest running drug trial in U.S. History (his story has never been given to any other journalist). I knew Jack was famous for being the personal pilot of drug lord Carlos Lehder, partner to Pablo Escobar, what I didn't know was that this former highflying smuggler would eventually divulge his deepest secrets to me, revealing, in his words, his *"true character"*. When Jack initially denied my request for information, I tossed his rejection letter aside figuring that was the end of it. Yet in a nanosecond, a voice in the back of my head insisted I respond immediately. I told Jack I respected his wishes, *"but... forgive me...I just feel compelled to reach out again—for what, I don't know!"* And this not knowingness was so very telling—because it underscored how intuitively and emotionally, we often understand more than we intellectually realize.

Jack admired my spunk, and amazingly, replied. Undeterred by my vagueness, Jack later revealed he had sensed I would have something to do with regaining his freedom, thus setting in motion the unexpected relationship that would change us forever. He also sensed a deep connection between us that pushes the limits of most common belief systems, implying a long-standing kinship at the soul level.

What Jack and I had in common was flying experience: his renegade, mine professional. As a pilot and journalist I decided my real interest was in wanting to hear about Jack's maverick flying adventures, and these he readily shared with me. And oh my God, was I ever enthralled! In his provocative flying escapades, Jack told me about his insatiable appetite for marijuana and wild sex, how he'd lived luxuriously on drug money, and the rush of living on the edge through the pampering of his senses. I asked for more stories please, Jack further indulged me, eventually sending me the memoir (originally entitled *PLAYA BLANCA, Escapades of a Buccaneer*) he had written years earlier. My. Jaw. Dropped. After reading it, I was consumed with a zillion questions. Jack answered them all and in time said I could be his biographer. *Buccaneer: The Provocative Odyssey of Jack Reed—Adventurer, Drug Smuggler and Pilot Extraordinaire* is the result.

When I met Jack, he was a 77—year old exemplary prisoner who had been languishing behind bars for twenty years and counting. Because he had refused to play ball with prosecutors, Jack told me how his constitutional rights were compromised. He told me about government wrong-doing in the courtroom that made my stomach turn. I know little about law, yet somewhere deep inside me, I knew Jack was not supposed to still be in prison—that his life sentence was a mistake that could be rectified and was past time to do so. Honestly, I don't know how I could know this but I did.

I began doing the background research for Jack's biography. This was to be a major turning point, because this would ultimately lead to the revelation that would change everything. It forced me to reach into the farthest depths of my soul to muster the courage to speak up for the man most everyone had forgotten. Courage I didn't even know I had—and swear I could not have summoned for myself! But for Jack—somehow I found the inner strength; and what I had to do scared me to death because it pushed me way out of my comfort zone.

It's hard to explain why I pushed myself to help him. It was the strangest thing. I never judged Jack nor questioned his crimes. I did not condone them, I just didn't judge. Frankly, had it been anyone else, I don't know if I could say that. As a journalist, I was eager to learn about the evolution of Jack Reed. I admired his courage to go against the grain of the conventional and expected societal norms and be his own man. I learned that his role as a drug smuggler came out of his genuine desire to provide a product that was in high demand and greatly appreciated by those that used it. Jack earned excellent income in doing so, thus affording him an adventurous anti-establishment lifestyle without the daily stress of worrying over the almighty buck. He told me he had no remorse about smuggling the products he considered similar to alcohol and tobacco. In Jack's mind, he was providing a service, plain and simple. It was a job. I never got the sense Jack did this to deliberately hurt anyone. That was not Jack's nature. He was a non-violent offender; a self-proclaimed pacifist; a caring tender soul who in no way resembled the cold-hearted bad boys convicts are often portrayed to be.

I was not attracted to Jack physically, although when we met, even at his advanced age, he was a still handsome and distinguished man. At 6'1", 170 pounds, with brown eyes and short salt and pepper hair, he was naturally fit. A stunner in his prime, this one—time tall, dark and handsome hippie playboy still possessed the magnetism that had attracted the many loves of his life.

Jack was twenty-five years my elder. I am ashamed to say it, but I had never really liked old people, especially old men. Horrible, I know; God, forgive me. While I am embarrassed to admit that, I am pleased to say I have since learned better; because with Jack, I eventually was able to see beyond the aging physical shell and recognize the eternal beauty beneath. There was an undeniable respect for and attraction to his spiritual essence; a knowing; a familiar safe haven; a distant connection that I couldn't put my finger on.

I must say that in addition to my driving need to take action on Jack's behalf, I felt a piercing unaccountable sadness, a heavy precognitive grief surrounding the yet unseen events that would unfold around Jack's final life adventure and my joining him on this path. My foresight of this mourning defied reason. Again, I say, intuitively and emotionally we often understand more than we intellectually realize. This angst would be buoyed by the stimulation of Jack sharing his spirited and soulful saga that mesmerized me like no other.

About a year and a half after Jack and I met, we would discuss the ballsy attributes of the prosecutors in his high profile trials. Jack mentioned what he really needed now was an attorney with similar chutzpah and big juice connections to win his freedom. I told Jack that 'Mad Dog' Robert Merkle had died years ago, but Ernst Mueller was still around in private practice. As Jack's former prosecutor, Mueller would not be a likely candidate to represent Jack now, but I was planning to contact him anyway to inquire about photographs for Jack's biography. Little did we know that my asking would be the magic ticket that would change everything —because when I approached Attorney Mueller—he was shocked to learn Jack was still in prison. He said he never considered Jack to be dangerous! That's right—he said he never considered Jack to be dangerous! There seemed to be a genuine concern for Jack in this former assistant U.S. Attorney.

It seems most everyone had forgotten about Jack, or assumed he'd been released a decade before. Jack later surmised that when Mueller heard that one of Jack's two life sentences had been vacated, he likely assumed the other one had been as well, mistakenly thinking Jack had ended up serving just his initial 15—year sentence.

I ask Mr. Mueller if he could possibly help us get the ball rolling to secure Jack's freedom. With Jack being a non-violent offender, and with his long history as an exemplary prisoner, this was most certainly do-able. And that's where the unexpected twist of fate comes in with the unlikely help from a surprising source—because Mr. Mueller agreed to help us!

Jack blesses me to move forward, commenting, *"You are gifted with what I consider amazing intuition/gut feeling. Not in a thousand years would I think that Ernst Mueller would have compassion for me. You may indeed have hit upon the miracle that we have been seeking. It is not the nature of prosecutors to be helpful to defendants. However, not having been one for several years, perhaps his sense of justice and mercy has mellowed his outlook... I think it's a great idea! Of course I support you in this effort 1000% and any assistance that I can provide is naturally yours for the asking! You're a genius...coming up with the idea of contacting Mueller about the photos. I never would have thought of it. I commend you on an excellent job and tell you that this is the best opportunity I have ever had. You are my champion."*

Who could have imagined that the very prosecutor who was instrumental in locking Jack up for life would eventually resurface to help free him now? On the sidelines, Mr. Mueller made the proper contacts to set the first necessary legal steps in motion. Being indigent, Jack was assigned a Federal Public Defender. Good things were happening. In addition, fellow inmate, close friend and jailhouse attorney, Gary Holt (Jack referred to previously)—who boasted an impressive winning track record helping inmates—had just assisted Jack in writing a new petition for Jack's release. It dealt with a disparity of sentencing issue that, if granted, would result in a reduction of Jack's sentence—setting him free. Very promising in addition to yet a previous motion—still not yet ruled on—Jack had filed two years earlier. It seemed that Jack, long overdue for a deserving break, may finally be rewarded for his unwavering faith and good behavior after all.

Things were moving forward—but at a snail's pace. Painstakingly slow because a life was hanging in the balance. A cancer Jack had been bravely battling quickly escalated into a terminal condition and it was later than we thought. What shocked me was the Bureau of Prisons (BOP) total disregard for a man's life—a precious life that was slipping away. No one seemed to be in a hurry to free Jack. He was just another prisoner serving time, although by now, he had been shipped to a Federal Medical

Center to pass away—still incarcerated—but in a prison hospital. A BOP representative there boldly told me that without question, an inmate with a natural life sentence, like Jack, was meant to die in prison. Period. End of story. He said that's the way it was intended to be, supposed to be, always had been, and will be. There was no room in this man's little mind for a miracle or a change in plans, even where a tragic sentencing mistake was at play. I felt disgust and empathy for him, and sadness that he worked in an environment where so many lives were soured by his rigid and closed mind.

This mindset was common throughout the prison system, all the way up to the highest ranking official. Fully acknowledging Jack's frail and terminal condition, at the last minute, the Director of BOP initially tried to block Jack's release, stating to the judge that he could not support it, mainly due to Jack's criminal history involvement with a large drug cartel. I found this disturbing and infuriating, until a good friend and fellow inmate of Jack's just recently reminded me that the notoriously violent reputation of the Medellin Cartel would most certainly prohibit the head of the BOP from blessing *any* former cartel associate to be set free. Of course the Director had no idea Jack had not even a fist fight to his credit, being non-violent to the bone.

Another government official—whose job included gathering certain legal documents necessary for Jack's release—was off on vacation. We would have to wait until he returned a week later. We didn't have a week! I kept protesting and nothing was moving fast enough. It seemed everything was in slow motion and either no one really understood the critical life and death time frame we were dealing with—or didn't care (after all, inmates die in prison all the time, remember?). Our Public Defender hated to give me the frustrating news of what seemed to be one delay and roadblock after another. I knew he wanted to help further, yet felt defeated and powerless to light a fire under the government's ass. That's when I departed my comfort zone and somehow found my voice and the strength to use it.

It was like pulling teeth to get the government to act quickly enough, but thanks to the grace of God, and screams of desperation to Mueller and our Public Defender, the judge granted Jack's freedom in the nick of time. Jack died just days later, a free man.

Freedom was all Jack ever wanted—so the fact that he was able to die a free man, with dignity – is a blessing beyond words. In addition, after a fifteen year estranged relationship with their father, Jack's daughters were by his side in his final days and when he drew his last breath, having reconciled their differences.

If you've been reading between the lines, you've likely gathered—in true form for this passionate maverick man who loved lust and being in love—Jack was able, once again, to *"pamper his senses"*, by finding love one last time. While Jack loved many women during his lifetime—*"all dearly"*, he told me, with a special love for Sheldon and the adventure they shared—I was to be Jack's last confidante and love interest. Never in a million years did I see this coming! It was a curve ball I never expected! In my role as Biographer, becoming privy to intimate details of Jack's intriguing life, our bond solidified. We adored one another. We were magic together and we knew it. And that's when our professional relationship evolved into a totally unexpected love story.

***

"If you press me to say why I loved him, I can say no more than because he was he, and I was I." —Michel de Montaigne

I am often asked what it was about Jack that made me fall in love with him, and if I wished I could have been in Sheldon's shoes—by Jack's side during his maverick adventure days on Norman's Cay and beyond. My answer to the latter is no. While I love Norman's Cay, having recently vacationed there dozens of times; back in the day of the drug operation, I was a young woman happily living out my own destiny as a fledgling television personality elsewhere. The fiery love affair Jack and Sheldon shared together was uniquely their own, and was meant for no one else. Although I find it titillating and intriguing, I have no longing for it.

The Jack I came to love, at the end of his life, was likely a different man. I fell in love with the evolution of Jack Carlton Reed. He was disciplined. I admired that. His ability to abstain from the pleasures of marijuana behind bars was impressive. The self-control to give up his beloved pot, knowing that by obediently following prison rules he'd have a better shot at his freedom—impressed me. By the time I came into Jack's life, he had evolved through years and years of spiritual and metaphysical studies. He'd had decades to meditate over his life behind bars, and was able to share that wisdom with me. Jack took full responsibility for creating his own reality; for his life choices and consequences; never a blaming a soul for his destiny. I respected that. His unwavering loyalty to his dear amigo Carlos, which he maintained to his dying day, was extraordinary. Jack was no rat! This was an important part of Jack's essence, and whether we understand that or not, matters not, because it's what made Jack *Jack*.

Behind bars, Jack grew into a gifted untrained artist and writer. There was a scholarly sophistication to him. He listened to classical music while painting with pastels. He loved *The*

Southern Cross by Crosby, Stills and Nash. Jack told me he was most grateful for the wonderful opportunity prison gave him in providing an education he never could have afforded on the outside. He said this learning event (prison) transformed him into a person he was proud to be. Highly intelligent and creative, Jack was a gentleman of strong faith with deep respect for his Creator. It was in prison, Jack tells me, where he discovered a spirituality within himself that he had been unaware of. This is not to be confused with religion, which Jack says he could never rationalize. His enduring faith in his freedom was inspiring. He never gave up, despite the fact he was locked into a life sentence! He was well respected by his fellow inmates and prison authorities alike. It appears he had outgrown any foolishness he may have harbored in his younger renegade days; but make no bones about it, the man had an edge. And I loved that about Jack. It was just the right amount.

Back in the '70's and 80's, Jack partied like a mad man with coke, weed, young girls and nefarious cartel people. Decades later, it was his self-control and spiritual maturity that seduced me.

"Seduce my mind and you can have my body, find my soul and I'm yours forever. ~ Anonymous

Jack was a wise soul who taught me about miracles and the power of love. He bestowed upon me an unfathomable love I never imagined I was capable of receiving or giving. I never even knew such love existed! And it was that love that pushed me well out of my comfort zone to spearhead his freedom. After Jack passed, I was contacted by two of his infamous high profile associates (still incarcerated) hoping I could help *them* gain *their* freedom. I had no interest. All I can say is that with Jack, it must have been a soul mate thing. Fate may have pre-ordained it.

Jack believed our meeting was destined. There were clues that seemed to affirm his premise. I had a muddled distant memory of knowing Jack from somewhere, yet was unable to grasp where.

It was a question I would ask Jack over and over again, *"Who are you?"* And his answer was always the same, *"Your soul mate."*

Jack and I had not met before, not in this lifetime. Any previous doubts we may have held about the possibility of reincarnation were now seriously in question. While I was consumed with confounded feelings (I had NEVER believed in soul mates before), Jack had a knowing all along who we were. We soon were propelled to move forward in getting (re)acquainted and on with our business that had been pre-ordained. And *Buccaneer—The Provocative Odyssey of Jack Reed, Adventurer, Drug Smuggler, and Pilot Extraordinaire* was the result. A compilation of the memoirs Jack wrote in prison and my personal notes taken from exclusive interviews and hundreds of letters and conversations shared between us in the final years of Jack's life. When we started our work together on this book, we had no idea how the story would end.

***

Life is eternal. Love never dies. Most of us who have lost a loved one *know* this, having felt the presence of the deceased loved one's spirit on occasion. Such is the case with Jack and me, as demonstrated time and time again through our close bond that lives on today.

Long before Jack passed, we were intimately tuned in to one another; sharing the ability to read each other's thoughts hundreds of miles apart. While I had always been somewhat empathic, my relationship with Jack amplified that; opening my heart. In fact, about eight months before Jack died, while he was being watched over 24/7 by prison guards as he lay shackled to a hospital bed, our mutual thoughts (telepathy or E.S.P. as Jack called it) kept us close. For security reasons, Jack was held at an undisclosed hospital (since he had been removed from the secure prison environment) where he underwent painful skin grafts after the removal of cancerous tumors. Because of Jack's former association with Carlos, and Pablo Escobar's notorious Medellin Cartel, Jack was held under tight security, with no phone privileges to call me, his dear sister, or anyone; this to hinder the possibility of his location leaking out. Perhaps prison officials feared the Cartel (long since defunct, and Pablo long dead and gone!) would send in the Colombian Cavalry to rescue Jack some twenty-two years after his capture—helping their long imprisoned smuggler escape! Seems ridiculous and abusive to subject a frail seventy-eight year old ailing and exemplary inmate to such treatment! Not only denying Jack access to the compassionate support of loved ones (the exception being my letters, addressed to Jack at FCI Memphis, which were hand delivered to Jack in the hospital by his prison counselor), but shackling Jack to the bed! Are you kidding me? Broke my heart. During that challenging time of great physical and mental anguish, Jack would later tell me, *"Without your love, life to me would be useless"*.

Months later, just weeks before Jack died, and we were waiting on the final paperwork for the judge to grant his release, I had a vision. I saw Jack standing tall and strong directly in front of me, wearing civilian clothes as opposed to his normal khaki prison garb. He looked intently at me with a generous smile and engaging wise eyes. He was healthy and clearly "restored" (by this time Jack had been confined to a wheelchair). He smiled wide and I knew the vision foretold one of two things: that he would recover and fully regain his health as a free man; or, he would succumb to the cancer, as his Doctors forecasted, but would be fully restored in Spirit. I shared this vision with Jack, wanting to assure him that whatever his fate, he would be just fine.

At the risk of further pushing the limits of most people's conventional beliefs, I will tell you that, since he passed, Jack has made his spiritual presence known to me on countless occasions over the years. I used to keep a journal of his messages and signs, but there have been so many, I have long since run out of pages. His communication and visitations (for lack of a better word) have brought me great comfort in demonstrating that love is eternal. Jack always warms my heart (while giving me the chills!) and provides beneficial guidance regarding my personal journey as well as our collaborative efforts on this book. He has even forewarned me about certain unsavory characters that deliberately disrespected his wishes after he died, and tried to interfere with our projects. Such attempts were foiled thanks to Jack's tip-offs that allowed me to protect myself.

While these encounters may be considered paranormal, they are not ghostly, scary or disturbing; although they did freak my dog out on more than one occasion.

I have grown through knowing Jack. He opened my heart. He taught me not to judge. To love unconditionally. While I don't agree with some of his choices, I am able to understand them through his eyes.

Regarding our love story, initially, I was hesitant to mention it—fearing it may discount my credibility as Jack's biographer; or detract from the other loves of Jack's life. But Jack insisted. It is important to him for everyone to know what we had was genuine. Jack's exact words.

The grief of Jack's passing still stings beyond words, but is soothed by the frequent presence of his sweet spirit. I can't begin to tell you how many tears have fallen on this keyboard as I have typed and retyped his biography over the past few years.

Like Jack said, he may be considered an adventurer by some, by others a damn fool. Regardless, what a ride he had! And at the end of it all, fully aware he had the power to create his own reality, Jack was rewarded with exactly as he had expected and had longed for—his freedom! It had been waiting for him all along in a bottomless well of undying love. A most fitting ending to the remarkable life of Jack Carlton Reed—an erotic adventure that had been filled with bountiful and boundless passion.

With Jack succumbing to cancer just days after his freedom was granted, I ache that he didn't have more time to embrace life outside prison walls. It is said when the soul gets what it came here to get, it goes. And Jack had to go.

Some of our last words to one another: *"My love for you is a journey; starting at forever, and ending at never"*. And that's what you call a storybook ending.

"One word frees us of all the weight and pain of life: That word is love". —**Sophocles**

ADDENDUM

A sampling of the hundreds of letters shared between Jack and MayCay during Jack's final years in prison.

SATURDAY· DECEMBER 22ND· 07

Dear Ms. Beeler

I am writing this very late response to your
missive that I received in August. Upon receipt
of your package & reading the first sentence
stating that you were working on a project
relating to "Return to Norman's Cay" - I read no
further - replaced the page in the package &
slipped it under my mattress - to be recovered
only this morning. It is not my nature to have
been so inconsiderate to you & not respond
before now - & my conscience motivated me
to take pencil in hand & apologize to you for
for my rudeness.

I have no excuse for my behavior except
that I have grown weary over the years of
my incarceration - being approached by authors -
TV producers - law enforcement - etc. to
participate in their various projects which
invariably adulterate the true story of
Norman's Cay - which very few are aware of.
This is still no excuse for not having
answered you immediately & I am sorry that
I am not motivated to become involved in
my infamous past history - preferring instead
to look to the future & the pursuit of my
art & literary endeavors.

I wish you good luck on your project &
stormless enroute flights in your flying machine

                    Respectfully· Jack Reed

③ SATURDAY - JULY 12TH '08

GOOD MORNING. I CAN'T MAIL THE PRECEEDING
UNTIL TOMORROW EVENING. SO I THOUGHT I WOULD
BORE YOU FOR A FEW MORE MINUTES.

SINCE WE HAVE MET & I BECAME AWARE OF WHAT
AN IMPORTANT PERSON YOU ARE IN MY LIFE. MY REALITY
HAS CHANGED NOTICEABLY. & I AM HAPPIER NOW THAN
I HAVE BEEN FOR MORE THAN TWENTY YEARS. YOU HAVE
BROUGHT INSPIRATION & PURPOSE INTO MY REALITY -
SIMILAR TO WHAT YOU ARE EXPERIENCING.

MY CREATIVE ACCOMPLISHMENTS HAVE BECOME MORE
APPARENT - WHICH IS VERY GRATIFYING. & I ATTRIBUTE
THIS TO YOUR POSITIVE ENERGY & INFLUENCE ON MY
THINKING. NEVER - IN MY LONG & DIVERSE LIFE HAVE
I HAD THE GREAT PLEASURE OF KNOWING A WOMAN
LIKE YOU. IN ALL OF MY RELATIONSHIPS - I STOOD
ALONE IN MY DESIRES & ACCOMPLISHMENTS - WITH MY
MATES CONTENT TO JUST BE ALONG FOR THE RIDE.
WITHOUT EXCEPTION - THEY WERE ALL LOVELY WOMEN
IN THEIR OWN SPECIAL WAY - BUT THEY LACKED THE
SPIRIT - IMAGINATION & DETERMINATION THAT YOU &
I POSSESS. IN OUR METAPHYSICAL JOURNEY
TOGETHER - YOU WILL DISCOVER - AS I DID - THAT
YOU & I BELONG TO A CERTAIN FAMILY OF SOULS
CALLED SUMARAI THAT HAVE PERSONALITY TRAITS
THAT WE HAVE IN COMMON. I CANNOT BE CONVINCED
THAT WE ARE NOT CLOSE SOULMATES & HAVE A BOND
THAT GOES MUCH DEEPER THAN OUR PRETENTIOUS
EGOS.

I AM LOOKING FORWARD TO A LONG & VERY HAPPY
RELATIONSHIP WITH YOU - MY VERY SPECIAL & LOVELY
FRIEND. VERY FEW SHARE THE FEELINGS THAT YOU &
I HAVE FOR EACH OTHER & I HAVE NO DOUBT THAT
WE WILL CONTINUE TO NURTURE THEM.

④

Egads MayCay - it's unbelievable what an effect you have on my well being / piece of mind. Just a few moments reflection on my good fortune of having your friendship & love overcomes all adver-sity. I have no words to describe how much you mean to me. I would give anything to be able to just hold you close & tenderly place a kiss on your soft beautiful cheek & feel your vibrant energy flow through my body. I have never felt such a desire to be with someone. My patience is wearing thin.

— SATURDAY —

Good morning sunshine - still locked down - but getting accustomed to the shabby treatment. With your energy surrounding me - I'll be okay.
I know that you are not happy about my treat-ment - & I considered not mentioning it to you - & destroying what I have written. I decided against it tho - because it is the sharing of my soul with you & portrays my sensitivity.

⑤

I want you to know the contrast of my feelings as a prisoner - sometimes feeling like a peaceful dove confined to a cage for the rest of my life - to the joy of finding a friend who cares about me - & wants to set me free - nurture me & be the recipient of the stored up love that I have to offer.
I know that you must sense that I consider you my savior - & that your compassion & love have captured my heart & soul - & that I now depend on you for the ultimate source of pampering my senses. You have my undying love for eternity. And those my beautiful friend - are my feelings for you.

— SUNDAY —

Still locked down. The warden is flexing his muscles. There is no longer a security problem.

A LOVE LETTER - TUESDAY - JULY 21ST - '09

DEAR MAYCAY -

I HAVE BEEN CONTEMPLATING THIS MISSIVE FOR SEVERAL DAYS NOW - TO SHARE WITH YOU MY DEEPEST THOUGHTS. I AM TROUBLED WITH DEEP CONCERN OVER MY INABILITY TO COMMUNICATE WITH YOU. AS YOU KNOW - CIRCUMSTANCES ARE & HAVE BEEN DICTATING THESE CONDITIONS - FOR THE MOST PART PLACING THEM BEYOND MY CONTROL - OR SO IT APPEARS.

OUR RELATIONSHIP WAS FOUNDED UPON OUR ABILITY TO COMMUNICATE CLEARLY WITH EACH OTHER - & ON THE BASIS OF OUR SPECIAL ABILITY TO DO THIS - A GREAT LOVE WAS ESTABLISHED. WE TRAVELED CALM PRISTINE SKIES WITH OUR DREAMS & FANTASIES - ESTABLISHING EXOTIC PARADISES & FORMIDABLE CHALLENGES - MANY - WHICH HAVE ALREADY BEEN SET INTO MOTION BY YOUR BRILLIANT EXPERTISE. EVERYTHING WAS POSITIVE & BOUND TO HAPPEN.

ALAS! ONE DAY - OUR SKIES TURNED DARK & TURBULENT. NEWS OF MY CRITICAL PERSONAL HEALTH CAUSED AN IMMEDIATE RELOCATION FOR SURGERY - WITH A NEED OF SECRECY FOR SECURITY REASONS RESULTING IN A TOTAL LACK OF COMMUNICATION FOR SEVERAL WEEKS. A DEVASTATING TURN OF EVENTS FOR BOTH OF US - AS IS THE NATURE OF TWO PEOPLE BEING DEEPLY IN LOVE. BECAUSE OF THE MORTALITY RATE - EVEN THO EVERYONE AVOIDS DISCUSSING IT - THE THOUGHT OF TERMINAL ILNESS PREVAILS - EVEN THO IN MY CASE NO DOCTOR HAS EVER MENTIONED IT. BLUS SKIES HAVE TURNED INTO THUNDER-STORMS - & EVEN SAFELY ON THE GROUND - APPREHENSION REIGNS SUPREME. LAYING SHACKLED IN MY HOSPITAL BED - HOOKED UP TO VARIOUS MACHINES - DRIPPING PUMPING & SUCKING - MY MIND - CLOUDED OVER BY ANASTHESIA & PAIN KILLERS - TRIES DESPERATELY TO INTERJECT A MOMENT OF PEACE - AN IMAGE OF YOU - THE ONE THAT I LOVE MORE DEARLY THAN ANYTHING - PERHAPS LIFE ITSELF - TO NO AVAIL. - MY ATTEMPT

FADING INTO OBSCURITY - SEEMING LIKE THE MEREST
POLLYANNA. I SHANT DWELL ON THESE TALES - FOR
YOU HAVE HEARD ENOUGH. I WISH THAT YOU HAD
NEVER BECOME AWARE OF THEM - ALLOWING ME
TO ABSORB ALL OF THEIR GRUESOME ENERGY.

DURING MY NIGHTMARES - OF COURSE - YOU STOOD
STEADFAST - SENDING LETTERS OF LOVE - ENCOURAGEMENT
& INSPIRATION - NOT KNOWING IF THEY WERE EVER
RECEIVED OR READ - BUT I'M WONDERING IF OUR
RELATIONSHIP WAS SUFFERING AS A RESULT OF THE
GRIEF WE WERE BOTH EXPERIENCING. CERTAINLY -
PROJECTS & DREAMS LOST SOME OF THEIR LUSTRE -
BUT WHAT ABOUT THE MOST IMPORTANT - THE LOVE?
I CRINGE TO THINK THAT THE PROFOUND LOVE THAT WE
EXPERIENCE IS SO DELICATE & WHIMSICAL - THAT IT ONLY
HAS SUBSTANCE DURING THE HIGHEST QUALITY OF LIFE.
ON THE CONTRARY. HAVING NOW EXPERIENCED THIS
SPLENDID EMOTION DURING BLUE SKIES & STORMS - I
CAN ONLY FEEL THAT IT HAS BEEN STRENGTHENED. I REMIND
YOU THAT THIS IS TOTALLY NEW TO BOTH OF US & HAS
NEVER BEEN EXPERIENCED BEFORE.

TODAY IS THE 30TH OF JULY - MORE THAN A WEEK
SINCE I STARTED THIS MISSIVE - AN EXAMPLE OF HOW
MY LACK OF ENERGY HAS SUPERCEDED ONE OF MY HIGHEST
PRIORITIES - WRITING LOVE LETTERS TO MY BEAUTIFUL BEST
FRIEND. TODAY - I FEEL A SLOW RECOVERY COMMENCING -
& I PLEAD TO IS THAT IT CONTINUES - SO THAT WE
MAY ONCE AGAIN EXPERIENCE OUR RELATIONSHIP
AS WE DID PRIOR TO THIS INTERRUPTION.

I AM DEEPLY BEHOLDING TO YOU FOR CARRYING THE
BURDEN OF COMMUNICATION DURING THIS TIME. YOU
HAVE NEVER FALTERED - STEADFASTLY CHEERING ME ON.
ALWAYS BUBBLING WITH LOVE - ENTHUSIASM & INSPIRATION.
MY BODY & MY SOUL ARE DEEPLY IN LOVE WITH YOU.

③

EVEN THO I HAVN'T SAID MUCH - I FIND MY
ENERGY WANING - BUT MUST PRESS ON & FINISH
THIS MISSIVE. YOU MUST KNOW HOW MUCH I
MISS YOU & LOVE YOU - THIS IS ALWAYS A CONSTANT
IT IS ONLY MY PRESENT LACK OF ENERGY THAT HAS
SLOWED ME FROM CONSTANTLY REMINDING YOU.
THIS TOO SHALL PASS - & ONCE AGAIN OUR FUTURE
WILL FLOURISH.

WHAT MORE CAN I SAY? YOU HAVE
NO DOUBT ABOUT HOW MUCH I ADORE YOU.

I HAVE ENOUGH ENERGY TO SEND TO YOU - JACK

In Reference to Federal Inmate Jack Carlton Reed, # 06844-018 FCI Memphis

August 24, 2009

The Honorable Timothy J. Corrigan
United States District Judge
Bryan Simpson United States Courthouse
300 North Hogan Street
Jacksonville, FL 32202

Your Honor,

This letter is of an urgent nature that respectfully begs your immediate attention.

I am writing, once again, on behalf of Jack Carlton Reed, an elderly inmate whose health is failing at an alarming rate. As a 78-year-old exemplary inmate, serving his 23rd year of a natural life sentence, Jack is facing a medical crisis that has provided a glaring wake-up call, revealing how fleeting and fragile life can be. Jack, and those who love him, now faces the realization that it may be later than we think.

After having already spent 16 weeks in the hospital so far this year, Jack finds himself hospitalized yet again. As I write this, he is scheduled to undergo a blood transfusion.

While recently struggling to recover from several surgeries for skin cancer, and from the harsh effects of extensive radiation while shacked to a hospital bed for three months, Jack, along with his loved ones (who are denied communication and visitation in an undisclosed hospital for security reasons), realizes it is past the time to formally ask for his freedom. For this reason, I come to you today in this second attempt to reach out to you with a heartfelt and soulful request for Jack's immediate release. Together with Jack and his family, I respectfully ask you to please grant him the privilege to live out his remaining time on this earth as a free man.

Decades ago, Jack worked as a pilot, smuggling drugs in the Bahamas. It was work that made sense to him at the time, doing so to earn income. It was never his intention to harm anyone. In fact, since having the privilege of getting to know Jack, I have found him to be a tender soul. Smuggling was a way to make a living plain and simple. When one knows better, they do better—and at that time, smuggling made sense to him.

As a result, Jack eventually faced a jury in what was to be the longest drug trial in U.S. History, alongside co-defendant Carlos Lehder. Because Carlos and Jack remained friends long after Jack retired from his smuggling days on Norman's Cay, it was assumed Jack was privy to business matters involving the Medellin Cartel. As Jack's Biographer and close friend, having gleaned some insight from Jack about his past, I am of the understanding that he was not. Jack was convicted of smuggling—that he was indeed guilty of; however, the charges involving alleged participation in continuing criminal enterprises had nothing to do with the reality of what involvement Jack did have with Carlos. While co-smugglers/associates testified against any and every one to win their own freedom or reduced sentences, Jack decided his friendship to Carlos was more important—and chose to keep his mouth shut about any personal insignificant details he did know.

The price Jack paid for this was his freedom. After two trials, he ended-up with two life sentences, due to Double Jeopardy and Ex Post Facto issues. One life sentence was vacated—and Jack is now living the autumn years of the second. Having no money, Jack never had the luxury of affording an ace attorney who could properly relate these sentencing errors to a judge. That is of little consequence now—as much water has passed under the bridge, taking with it Jack's youth.

Jack is not a violent or evil person. The staff at FCI Memphis can tell you he is an exemplary prisoner. Jack tells me that long ago, after accepting his fate "as a bird with clipped wings in a cage", he decided, "It was best to follow the rules, and not resist this institution or my keepers". Even Jack's original prosecutor, Ernst Mueller, has expressed concern—saying he "never considered Jack dangerous, and that it seems useless that he still be in jail at this late stage in his life."

Jack has made every effort to make the best of his confined life experience in an honorable way. He tells me, "I am pleased to say I am proud of the person I have become. I have learned more than I could have ever imagined though my education in prison." Jack has evolved into a pacifist/philosopher/artist over the decades, studying countless books on Faith. They have sustained him through what many consider a life without hope—a natural life sentence. Jack values the deep spirituality he has gleaned from his life experience as an inmate, and relates, "I am grateful for it."

However, the time has now come, as Jack approaches age 79 in ailing health, when he longs for a last opportunity to enjoy life and die a free man. He is deserving of this last chance to live out his life free of prison walls, and heal in a loving environment.

Jack was estranged from his daughters for years, yet now they are back in his life with a sincere desire to accept their wayward father. They pray for the opportunity for their Dad to come home to them where they can provide the proper nutrition and TLC he sorely needs to heal. In addition, my own relationship with Jack has grown quite close in the most caring of ways. It is my intention, for as long as Jack desires, to love and nurture this dear man upon his release.

Jack is not a threat to anyone. He says he has learned invaluable lessons in his 22-plus years in prison—about God, the Universe, and Life. The possibility of a last chance to know love once again—first hand—through family and a good woman—is a priceless gift that I know Jack will respect and cherish every minute of every day in his time remaining. Therefore, I respectfully ask you, Honorable Sir, to please grant the freedom that will enable Jack to fully embrace this last precious opportunity. Thank you so very much for your time and consideration of our ardent request. Time is short. He is fading. Please help us, Sir.

Respectfully,

MayCay Beeler, on behalf of Jack Carlton Reed, #06844-018 FCI Memphis

Dfb.c/o Counsel

UNITED STATES DISTRICT COURT
MIDDLE DISTRICT OF FLORIDA
JACKSONVILLE DIVISION

UNITED STATES OF AMERICA

vs.

CASE NO. 3:89-cr-29-J-32MCR

JACK CARLTON REED

ORDER

Yesterday, the Court issued an Order (Doc. 1607) requesting the Director of the Bureau of Prisons to reconsider his position as to the request for compassionate release of defendant Jack Carlton Reed. Upon review of that Order, and in light of additional information, the Director has now advised the Court that he "will not object to a reduction of [Mr. Reed's] sentence."[1]

Accordingly, upon due consideration, and pursuant to 18 U.S.C. § 3582(c)(1)(A)(i), the Court's September 29, 2009 Order granting the Director's motion for sentence reduction and directing the Bureau of Prisons to immediately release Jack Carlton Reed (Doc. 1603) is hereby **REINSTATED** such that:

1.   Defendant Jack Carlton Reed's previously imposed sentence of imprisonment for a term of Life is now reduced to **time served**;

2.   Defendant Jack Carlton Reed shall be **immediately released** from the custody of the Bureau of Prisons to Mr. Reed's family;

3.   If Mr. Reed is discharged from the hospital, the previously arranged release

---

[1]The Clerk shall file the Director's letter so that it will be of record.

plan approved by the United States Probation Office (which plan included provision for

defendant's supervised release) shall take effect at that time.

     DONE AND ORDERED in Jacksonville, Florida, this 9th day of October, 2009.

                                        TIMOTHY J. CORRIGAN
                                        United States District Judge

s.
Copies:
Julie Hackenberry Savell, Esq. (AUSA -Jax)
James H. Burke, Jr., Esq. (Asst. Fed. Def. -Jax)
United States Probation Office
U.S. Marshal Service
Bureau of Prisons
   and by facsimile to David Huband, Esq.
Defendant

2

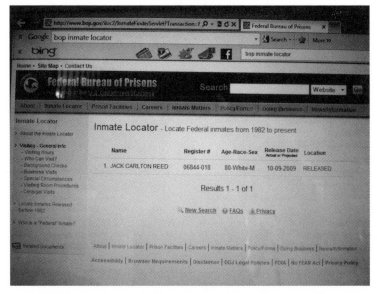

Bureau of Prisons Inmate Locator website screen shot

From the *Long Beach Press Telegram*, Saturday, August 7, 1971

Electric Car in Speed Mark

Wendover, Utah (UPI)—The bullet-shaped Silver Eagle Friday set a world land speed record for electric cars of 146.437 miles per hour, using the same type batteries which powered the Apollo 15 Lunar Rover.

Jack Reed, 40, of Huntington Beach, Calif., guided the sleek racer, powered by 180 silver-zinc powered cells, through the flying mile on the Salt Flats Raceway two times, setting the record plus a one-way record of 152.355 mph.

Reed said the crew could have eclipsed the old mark of 134.45 mph by "considerably more, but bad track conditions forced us to make short approach runs".

Reed said the 183-inch long racer could only use the miles of track at the north end and only two miles at the south end before hitting the timers in the measured mile.

The batteries, manufactured by Eagle-Picher Industries, Inc., Joplin, Mo., powered the racer to 20 other records in two different weight classes, depending on the configuration of the car.

ACKNOWLEDGEMENTS

First and foremost, although he is not physically here to read it, I cannot begin to thank Jack enough for sharing his remarkable and controversial story, and for the joy of our collaborative efforts in telling it. Jack's stunning loyalty to his beloved comrade Carlos, and unwavering faith in his own freedom, is inspirational beyond words.

My deepest thanks to the late Ernst Mueller and Federal Public Defender James H. Burke, Jr., who helped bring an end to the prison sentence that had haunted Jack for nearly twenty-three years.

Special heartfelt thanks to Aaron K. Sharpe for his invaluable help, encouragement and ongoing support, as well as Nate Wright, Gary and Stephanie Holt; all have gently and lovingly guided me in Jack's absence.

I am grateful to the following that have nourished me throughout this project: Julie Milunic, Greg Gibson, Elizabeth Wolf, Leslie Manheim, Heidi Novak, Robert Patton and Bradley Smith.

Thanks to Ron Chepesiuk, Dimas Harya, and Sheree Alderman whose votes of confidence and support flew to me on Angel's wings; Jeffrey Reichard, Robert Tompkins; Mary Margret Daughtridge; Rusty Sharpe; Craig Peyton, Sidney Kirkpatrick; Stefan Paton; Bruce Griffin; Delbert Fentress; William Mangum; Bill Johnson; and Bill Hall.

Very special gratitude to Dick and Gene Fayssoux, and Dempsey and Vi Clinard, who would unknowingly lead me to Jack through the research I conducted for the TV Documentary I produced about their crash landing on Norman's Cay.

And lastly, I am grateful to my son, RJ, for his love and support through-out.

Jack Carlton Reed, (September 30, 1930 – October 12, 2009) was a convicted drug smuggler and co-defendant of Carlos Enrique Lehder Rivas, Colombian drug baron and partner to Pablo Escobar of the Medellín Cartel. Reed was a pilot working under Lehder's cocaine transport empire on Norman's Cay, an out island 210 miles off the Florida coast in the Bahamas. Reed flew drug runs for Lehder who handled transportation, while Colombian drug lord Escobar handled production and supply.

Provocative and controversial, nonconformist Jack Reed was a daring adventurer and maverick entrepreneur. He loved love, lust, erotica and passion—living riveting adventures larger than life. A career as a professional high flying international cocaine smuggler for the Medellin Cartel landed this renegade pilot behind bars in a draconian life sentence that was a tragic judicial mistake. A non-violent offender, Jack was severely punished for refusing to snitch on close friend Carlos Lehder.

Jack was happiest living a simple anti-establishment self-reliant lifestyle as an expat in tropical seclusion. A modern day buccaneer, Jack was allergic to the drudgery of the establishment. He described himself as "a*n eccentric old pirate*" and "*hedonistic philosopher*", going against the grain of the expected societal norms he found suffocating. During nearly twenty-three years of incarceration, Jack evolved into a disciplined student of metaphysics. In addition to this faith, painting would become his lifeline. An untrained artist who discovered his hidden talent behind bars, Jack created an impressive portfolio of pastel paintings while serving life in prison. While Jack's art work is remarkable in itself, consisting of photograph life-like images, it is the colorful provocative history of the artist himself that is most enthralling. Jack's legacy lives on through his art and memoirs. See www.jackcarltonreed.com.

Credit: Sara Anne Photography

MayCay Beeler is an American world record-breaking professional pilot, published author, and award-winning TV Personality. As a veteran TV Host/Producer/Journalist, she has worked for every major Network TV affiliate in News and Entertainment television for 30 years and counting. She is a champion of aviation and an active FAA Certified Flight Instructor. Visit www.maycaybeeler.com.

"Have I Told You Lately"

"Have I told you lately that I love you
Have I told you there's no one else above you
Fill my heart with gladness
take away all my sadness
ease my troubles that's what you do

"For the morning sun in all it's glory
greets the day with hope and comfort too
You fill my life with laughter
and somehow you make it better
ease my troubles that's what you do
There's a love that's divine
and it's yours and it's mine like the sun
And at the end of the day
we should give thanks and pray
to the one, to the one

"Have I told you lately that I love you
Have I told you there's no one else above you
Fill my heart with gladness
take away all my sadness
ease my troubles that's what you do

"There's a love that's divine
and it's yours and it's mine like the sun
And at the end of the day
we should give thanks and pray
to the one, to the one

"And have I told you lately that I love you
Have I told you there's no one else above you
You fill my heart with gladness
take away my sadness
ease my troubles that's what you do
Take away all my sadness
fill my life with gladness
ease my troubles that's what you do.
Take away all my sadness
fill my life with gladness
ease my troubles that's what you do."

-Rod Stewart

"Follow You Follow Me"
"Stay with me,
My love I hope you'll always be
Right here by my side if ever I need you
Oh my love

"In your arms,
I feel so safe and so secure
Everyday is such a perfect day to spend
Alone with you

"I will follow you will you follow me
All the days and nights that we know will be
I will stay with you will you stay with me
Just one single tear in each passing year

"With the dark,
Oh I see so very clearly now
All my fears are drifting by me so slowly now
Fading away

"I can say
The night is long but you are here
Close at hand, oh I'm better for the smile you give
And while I live

"I will follow you will you follow me
All the days and nights that we know will be
I will stay with you will you stay with me
Just one single tear in each passing year there will be

"I will follow you will you follow me
All the days and nights that we know will be

I will stay with you will you stay with me
*Just one single t*ear in each passing year..."

–Genesis

INDEX

CURRENT AND FORTHCOMING TITLES FROM
STRATEGIC MEDIA BOOKS

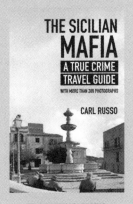

SPY OF DAVID
The Strange Case of Jonathan
Pollard and The Two Decade Battle
to Win His Freedom

THE SICILIAN MAFIA
A True Crime Travel Guide

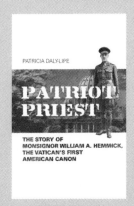

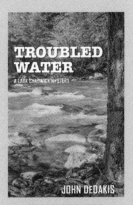

PATRIOT PRIEST
The Story of Monsignor William
A. Hemmick, The Vatican's First
American Canon

TROUBLED WATER
A Lark Chadwick Mystery